LIVING A
CHAMPIONSHIP
LIFE

LIVING A
CHAMPIONSHIP
LIFE

A Game Plan
for Success

DR. RICK GOODMAN

© Copyright 2008 Dr. Rick Goodman
ISBN: 978-0-9795737-7-4

Library of Congress Control Number: 2008903975

Book Production: SPS Publications
Eustis, Florida. www.spsbooks.com

Design: Jessica Mitchem

Published by: Anzman Publications
7247nw 22nd Drive, Pembroke pines, Florida 33024
www.Anzmanpublishing.com

DEDICATION

To Alex, Jamie, and Jackie
You are my strength.
I love you more than the universe!

*In Loving Memory of my father Norman Joel Goodman,
who taught me the one lesson that has had the greatest
impact on my life: "Goodmans Don't Quit."*

CONTENTS

A.S.K.

Mirroring and Modeling Techniques

Communicating Your Goals and Explain Your Needs

Check Back Your Key to Delegation Success

The Disease Called Constructive Criticism

Paraphrasing Your Key to Understanding

That's Not Like You

Communication Techniques for Dealing with Difficult People

The Three F's

Living a Championship Life Action Step 7

Faith

Forgiveness

Blocked Energy

The Forgiveness Letter

Gratitude

Creating Magic Moments

Health and its Importance in Becoming a Champion

Minimize Pressure and Handle Stress with Relaxation Techniques

Learn to Laugh

Leaders motivate and inspire—they relentlessly create the vision and set strategies for ACTION. Their ultimate gift is not to have followers, but to develop many other leaders.

– Dr. Rick Goodman

ACKNOWLEDGMENTS

The evolution of this book has taken ten years to hash out. Over this time technology and the way the world operates have undergone massive change. While change is always present, the one stability I have had during that period of time has been the stability of my family and friends. I want to thank my grandparents, Mimi and Pop, for teaching me many lessons about life and the importance of family. Mimi, your insight into people and human nature shows the wisdom of the ages, and I appreciate your sharing that with me so that I may share it with others.

To my mom, Linda Berman, who has always been there to listen with a kind word and a smile upon her face. To my Aunt Roni and Uncle Ivan Senzon, you've been a voice of reason in times of chaos, which is always appreciated along life's highway of ups and downs.

I would also like to extend a special thanks to Tony Ruesing and Shep Hyken, who have been with me on this road from the beginning, encouraging me and mentoring me throughout my journey. Your guidance, friendship, and insight helped me to grow personally and professionally.

I would also like to acknowledge my sixth grade friends. People I meet in my programs and at home can't believe that I have kept in touch with people for such a long time. Being a professional speaker enables me to do just that. Alicia Rosenfeld, Jeff Coyle, Mike Dicks, and Richie the kid Culligan—you have all taught me what true friendship is all about. To the Anzman Clan my sisters Audrey, Lori and my brother John and my cousins Jack, Simon and Michelle you have taught me about family and when we all get together it still seems like camp. A special thanks to Brad Rabinowitz whose ideas for the title of this book convinced me to look at success from a different perspective enabling anyone to "Live a Championship Life." Also Bruce Turkel and Will Ezell who are always honest with me about life as they teach me about the wonderful world of marketing and branding, and to Ford Saeks, who has shown me the ropes regarding the wonderful world of the Internet.

Most of all my best friend and brother in life, Mitch Less, who's been with me through thick and thin, providing guidance and support that only a best friend and brother could do. Our trips abroad have created memories that will last a lifetime. And I wish everybody could have the friendship and bond that we have enjoyed for so many years.

I would also like to thank my children Alex and Jamie for being the best kids a father could ever ask for. You make me laugh and you make me cry—from tears of joy. You have also taught me lessons about the importance of family and balance, and how important it is to be a kid. I could ask for nothing more!

Lastly and mostly, I would like to thank my wife, Jackie, who's the strongest woman I know. Your zest for life and support of me and all things I strive for, inspires me to touch more people's lives and make a difference. You are my rock!

Finally, thanks to Bruce Feustel, Jessica Mitchem, and Dennis Schick at SPS Publications, for their professional talents and skills in bringing this labor of love to the product you hold in your hands.

INTRODUCTION

Millions of people every year get together on one special day in sports—the Super Bowl. In fact, it is the single most-watched sporting event in the world. But there are other "big" days in other sports, as well. Consider March Madness, the NBA Championship and the Final Four for college basketball. How about the National Championship in college football, or the Stanley Cup in hockey? Then there are the Olympics—Summer and Winter—the World Cup (soccer), and the World Series. All represent excellence in sports, and in life!

Have you ever wondered what makes an organization successful? What are the defining principles that can take an organization from mediocrity to success, and how can I apply the same principles to my organization?

The good news is, successful individuals, corporations, and sports franchises all utilize time-tested principles of communication—teamwork, time management, motivation, and overall balance—to accomplish goals and objectives.

The more I have studied success, the more I have found a correlation between successful businesses, individuals, and world champion sports teams. In 1995, the Los Angeles Rams of the

National Football League moved to St. Louis, and I had the opportunity to be one of the doctors for the team. In addition, I was on the medical staff of the St. Louis Ambush, the former champions of the Major Professional Indoor Soccer League.

Many of the principles that I observed in the five years that I worked with the Rams players, watching them go from a losing team in all aspects of the game, to become the Super Bowl champions, can be applied to your business and life.

I've included these principles and many more I have observed and implemented while working with organizations like AT&T, Hewlett-Packard, Boeing, and all branches of the United States armed forces.

My goal and dream for you is that you are able to apply these principles to your life. When you do, you will find that you will have more balance and less stress, and a game plan to achieve all your goals and dreams. The principles in this book will put you well on your way to living a championship life!

CHAPTER 1
ATTITUDE IS EVERYTHING!

It's been said many times that your attitude will determine your altitude. You can only achieve those things that you truly believe in your mind that you can achieve.

Well here's the good news—you can change your attitude if you know how your attitude is formed. Your attitude is shaped primarily by your experiences. If you've had positive experiences, most likely your attitude will be positive; and, conversely, if you've had negative experiences, most likely your attitude will be negative.

To give you an example, one of my mentors, Dr. Larry Markson, would say, "Your attitude is shaped by your MFTP." Your MFTP—your mother, father, teacher, and preacher—shaped many of your belief systems. If you think about it, how often have you ever heard these statements: "Children should be seen and not heard," "Don't speak until spoken to," or maybe the ever-popular, "Rich people are thieves?" Unfortunately, many of us have heard those statements, and for a few of us, this is our reality.

Again, you can change this if you have a basic understanding of how attitudes are formed. Think about your experiences as if they were a table. The top of the table is your experience and the legs of the table are your references. If you've had a whole bunch of positive references for most of your life, you're probably going to have positive experiences. On the other hand, if you've had a whole bunch of negative references, most likely your experiences are going to be negative.

But remember that you can change that! You can change your experience by changing your attitude of mind. Now I know that sounds pretty simple, but the truth of the matter is that it's going to take practice and take some time.

In 1995, Los Angeles Rams owner Georgia Frontiere decided to move her National Football League (NFL) team back to her hometown of St. Louis, Missouri. The Rams' first few years in St. Louis were as bad as their final years in Los Angeles. Rich Brooks was hired as the coach to turn the team around. He had been a longtime successful football coach at the University of Oregon.

When the team moved to St. Louis, it played its first few games at Busch Stadium, winning five out of their first six. Then the old negative attitudes started to creep in, and the team went 2-8 for the rest of the season, missing the playoffs again. After two more terrible seasons, Rich Brooks was fired and replaced by Dick Vermeil.

Vermeil had enjoyed success as the head coach at UCLA, where his team won the Rose Bowl, and with the Philadelphia Eagles, leading them to victory in Super Bowl XV. Anybody who has seen the movie *Invincible* with Greg Kinnear and Mark Wahlberg, can get a sense of the positive attitude that Vermeil exudes with his players and coaches alike.

I have a saying—"Teams go where you go." Once you make a decision to change your attitude on a daily basis, you will begin to notice things changing around you. How you think and what you think about on a regular basis determines your outcome. Now I know this sounds a little crazy so let me give you an example:

Have you ever been in a rush to leave work so that you wouldn't be late for an appointment? How many red lights did you get stopped at? I bet I know the answer—every single one! Now when you left the office you knew you were going to be in a rush and you said to yourself, "Please don't let me hit all those red lights," and because that's where your energy was going, that's what you attracted. You got stopped at every red light! It's all about attitude! You attracted exactly what you did not want by focusing on it intently.

Getting back to the Rams, Vermeil's first two seasons were as unsuccessful as many of the seasons that preceded it. I remember many times, when players would come into my office to get treated, you would think that they were not only happy about the losing, but they were resolved to it.

Some of my non-sports patients would see the negative attitudes demonstrated by the players coming into our waiting room on a daily basis, and they also began to give up on the team. Some even began to ask me if I could do anything about it, that maybe there was a special treatment that I could perform that would heal them and fix their attitudes. I reminded them that success and health were both inside jobs, and the only person who truly has control over health and success is ourself.

Then in 1999, the Rams acquired quarterback Trent Green and running back Marshall Faulk in two separate trades, and the city of St. Louis felt like this would finally be the turning point for the Rams.

Unfortunately in the third preseason game, quarterback Green was knocked to the ground, tearing up his knee, ending his season. The city of St. Louis was in mourning, once again looking forward to another losing season.

But then something dramatic happened. An individual, who knew no bounds—with an attitude of gratitude for just being able to play the game—took over as the starting quarterback. Kurt Warner.

Warner is somebody who's always made the most of the chances given to him. At the University of Northern Iowa, Warner watched two quarterbacks battle for the starting position until his senior year. He hung in there and didn't give up until he was finally given a chance to start in his last season. In that year he was named the Gateway Conference Offensive Player of the Year.

He attended the Green Bay Packers training camp in 1994 but was released before the regular season began. He then returned to Northern Iowa and worked as a graduate assistant coach with the football team, never giving up hope to get a tryout with an NFL team.

Working at a grocery store stocking shelves, with no NFL teams wanting to take a chance on him, Warner turned to the Arena Football League, signing with the Iowa Barnstormers.

All along, Warner maintained a positive attitude, while leading the team to Arena Bowl appearances in 1996 and 1997. He was also named as one of the twenty best Arena Football players of all time.

In 1997, Warner was offered an NFL tryout by the Chicago Bears. But an injury to his throwing elbow caused by a venomous spider bite received during his honeymoon, prevented him from attending training camp. At the time it seemed like nothing was going right for him.

Warner was signed by the St. Louis Rams, and they promptly sent him to NFL Europe's Amsterdam Admirals. By this point, if you were Kurt Warner you might be thinking it's time to give up!

I've studied successful individuals in sports and industry alike, and I have found that there is a common principle that keeps them from giving up and enables them to rise above circumstances and situations that would stop most people.

They all possess a **positive mental attitude**, and they **never give up**! Well, by now you probably know the rest of the story. When Trent Green went down with a season-ending knee injury, Kurt Warner took over as the starting quarterback of the St. Louis Rams, leading them to the Super Bowl championship in his first season, and being named both the NFL MVP, and the MVP of Super Bowl XXXIV.

Self Image and Its Effect on Your Attitude:

Self-image is defined as one's concept of oneself and one's own identity. To make it real simple, it is how we perceive ourselves when we wake up in the morning and look in the mirror every day.

The question is do you like what you see when you look in the mirror, because it's going to have a positive or negative effect on your success in life.

Those people who possess a poor self-image tend to be under-achievers, blaming the circumstances in their lives on outside forces other than themselves. They tend to criticize other people, making excuses—blaming their school, their parents, and any other forces in their life for their negative condition. Many of them have a victim mentality and ask the same question over and over—"Why me?"

Unfortunately, for many people who possess a poor self-image, they ask themselves that question, and get an answer back from their brain that they don't want to hear. On the flip side, those people who possess a positive self-image tend to be the over-achievers in life, constantly attracting opportunities that will help them to get ahead and fulfill their destiny.

John Wooden, the world-renowned college basketball coach at UCLA, who led his team to ten NCAA championships over a twelve-year span, said, "Do not let what you cannot do interfere with what you can do." It's important for us to focus on the opportunities we have in life and on the things that we have control over, not outside forces or circumstances.

Both Kurt Warner and Dick Vermeil demonstrated what a positive mental attitude and an outstanding self-image can do for a football team. Just think about what it can do for you!

Techniques for Improving Your Attitude and Building Your Self-Image

There are two techniques that I have found to be essential in improving your attitude and building your self-image. The first is the power of **Affirmations**. An affirmation is a positive statement that you recite to yourself or out loud that represents an experience or behavior that you would like to attain.

Years ago I read a book called *Psycho Cybernetics*, by Dr. Maxwell Maltz. In the book he stated, "The mind does not know the difference between something actually happening and something that was imagined vividly and in great detail." Other motivational speakers have said, "Act as if," and "Fake it until you make it." I don't think that they were saying that you should be a phony, but that you should act in a manner congruent with the person that you want to become.

I have been using affirmations, since I learned about them in 1988, and it has been a life- transforming experience for me.

One day, I was sitting in class listening to a very successful doctor talk about what it took to be successful. He said there are three types of people in this world. The first is the type of person who dreamed all day long about what they were going to do and they never moved out of the lotus position. Then there was the type of person who talked about what they were going to do with visions of grandeur dancing in their heads. Finally, there was the person who took massive action, who did whatever they said they were going to do.

When he said this, it had a profound effect upon me and my focus for the future. I wasn't going to be that person in the lotus position. I was going to be the person who took massive action! Which person are you going to be?

The Power of Affirmations:

The doctor then spoke about the **power of affirmation**, and how it changed his life. He didn't have to sell me any longer on the idea. He was a successful doctor, he was driving a Porsche, he had a big practice, and he had a brand-new house. I thought if he can do that, so could I.

That night I was reading a book called *Successful Achievement* by Sidney N. Bremer, Ph.D. He described the story of Dr. Orison

Swett Marden, the founder of *Success* magazine. When I read this quote I knew what my affirmation would be. It said, "Constant affirmation increases courage, and courage is the backbone of confidence. Furthermore, when a person gets in a tight place and says, 'I must,' 'I can,' 'I will,' he not only reinforces his courage and strengthens his confidence, but also weakens the opposite qualities."

Since that point in time, I have repeated this same affirmation every day: **I must, I can, I will!** This simple affirmation is one of the most powerful techniques that you can use to help you develop a positive can-do attitude about any experience and situation.

Focus on Your Strengths

The more we focus on the things that we are good at, the better we feel about ourselves. When we focus on our strengths, our strengths will grow, and when we focus on our weaknesses, unfortunately they will grow also.

In order to "live a championship Life" we need to know what our strengths are and continually work on them. The Super Bowl Champion St. Louis Rams knew that their strength was speed. They were known as The Greatest Show on Turf and they used their strength and speed as their ultimate weapon to beat their opponents. They would strike within seconds of the opening kick-off, running teams out of the stadium, and they often won games by more than twenty points.

If you want to be successful in your personal life and professional life it's important that you understand where your strengths lie. Ask yourself these questions: What are my strengths? What am I good at? What do I love to do? When you answer these questions, you will most likely have discovered your strengths, because those are the things that you are really good at and truly love to do.

I was watching the *Tonight Show* with Jay Leno, and he was interviewing the actor Samuel Jackson. Jackson was talking about how much fun he had in life making movies, playing golf, and chasing his dreams. I then focused on what Jackson said next. Leno posed the question, what is the secret to your success?

Jackson replied, "The more you do what you love, the more fun you have, the more money you will make."

To me this was a profound statement. If you're not doing what you truly love to do then why continue doing it? You will never be successful if you continue on that road. When we truly find a way to do what we love to do, our dreams will turn into reality and we will attract all that we want out of life!

When Dick Vermeil was coaching the Philadelphia Eagles, he was asked how he felt about coaching. Vermeil said. **"After I got my Masters Degree, I still loved the game so much, I went into coaching, and stayed with it. My hobby is my work; I love it so much it's not work."**

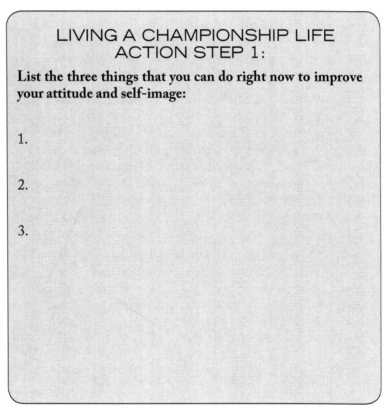

LIVING A CHAMPIONSHIP LIFE
ACTION STEP 1:

List the three things that you can do right now to improve your attitude and self-image:

1.

2.

3.

CHAPTER 2
YOUR GAME PLAN
FOR SUCCESS

Every great Super Bowl championship football team has had a game plan for success during the regular season, as well as for the playoffs, and for the championship game.

In the 1999 Super Bowl season, the St. Louis Rams instituted their game plan, which was closely aligned with the goals that they had set at the beginning of the season. Coach Dick Vermeil was known for his goal-setting methods and motivational style of leadership.

If you were to go to Rams Park in Earth City, Missouri, you would notice in the meeting rooms the long list of goals. The goals were broken down by individual game statistics, including rushing yards, passing yards, time of possession, giveaways and takeaways, and many more.

There were offensive goals, defensive goals, and special teams goals. Everything was accounted for, and each player knew what his responsibility was and what was expected from him.

In the Super Bowl, the Rams game plan was to put the ball in the hands of Kurt Warner, their MVP quarterback, and Marshall Faulk, the NFL offensive player of the year.

The goals that were the foundation of the Rams season helped to lead them to victory in the 1999 Super Bowl. Kurt Warner had an outstanding game and was named the Most Valuable Player, completing twenty-four passes for four hundred and fourteen yards and two touchdowns. Marshall Faulk had one hundred and seven yards of total offense and receivers Isaac Bruce and Torry Holt both had touchdowns and each went over one hundred yards receiving.

Goals your roadmap and game plan for success

The single most important thing that you and I can do to live a championship Life is to set goals. Your goals are your roadmap and your game plan for success. Studies have shown that only ten percent of people on this planet set goals. These are the top achievers—the people in this world who are going places, touching lives, and having fun!

Since 1988 I have been using a goal-setting system that has been used by thousands of successful people around the world and I would like to share it with you. If I could give you the key to unlock the door to a more prosperous and healthy life would you be interested? Recently I was giving a seminar and I decided to ask the audience one of my favorite life questions. I looked around at all the people in the room and asked: **What do you want to be when you grow up?**

The response I received by the majority of the audience was the same one that I had received countless times previously—**"I don't know!"** This answer has always perplexed me since it seemed that most people were waiting for life to happen to them as opposed to designing and creating their ideal life. The common dilemma that most people face is they really have no idea what they want. They also have no practical way to create a plan and put it into action to achieve their goals.

S.M.A.R.T System of Goal Setting

Since 1988 I have been using a simple method of goal setting that has worked for me and I know it will work for you. It is called the **S.M.A.R.T. System of Goal Setting**. It is an acronym for:

Specific

Measurable

Achievable /Attainable

Realistic

Time Specific

Each one of your goals must meet these criteria and have these basic components. In addition, it is important that you break down your goals to cover five specific areas of your life:

1.Career/Financial

2. Developmental/Educational

3. Physical/Health

4. Family/Relational/Social

5. Spiritual/Value

Now that you have an understanding of the S.M.A.R.T. System and the areas that you should be covering, let's break down the system into ten easy steps that you can implement immediately, from which you can enjoy the benefits for the rest of your life.

Step 1:

Take a lined pad of paper and write down everything that you want to Be, Do, and Have. These are your goals.

Step 2:

Make sure that your goals can meet the criteria of the S.M.A.R.T. System.

Step 3:

Create goals that will cover the five specific areas that we discussed.

Step 4:

Put your written list of goals away for twenty-four hours before you review it.

Step 5:

Review your goals and put them to the test by asking yourself the following questions.

- Is this goal something I really want?
- Is this a fair goal that won't affect anyone in a negative way?
- Do my goals align with my ethical and moral standards?

Step 6:

Eliminate any goals that do not meet these criteria. The remaining goals should be the ones you focus your attention on.

Step 7:

Review your goals three times daily—when you wake up, during the day, and when you go to bed.

Step 8:

Each day, plan action steps designed to move you closer to achieving your written goals.

Step 9:

Consistently monitor and measure your progress in order to stay on track of your goals and make the appropriate adjustments.

Step 10:

Celebrate your achievements.

Stephen R. Covey, the author of *Seven Habits of Highly Effective People,* first published in 1989 and which has sold over fifteen million copies in thirty-eight languages since its first publication, discusses his concept of long-term goal setting in his chapter "Begin with the End in Mind."

Covey recommends formulating a **"personal vision statement"** to document one's perception of one's own vision and life. He sees visualization as an important tool to develop this. He also deals with organizational vision statements, which he claims to be more effective if developed and supported by all members of an organization rather than just prescribed. If you have not read this book yet, I highly recommend it. If you want to live a championship life, you need to have an idea of what you want to achieve in life and where you want to go.

There is another technique that I use to set goals that is very effective. I find that most people have a difficult time formulating their goals for one of two reasons, time or money. Most of the people I spoke with did not feel that they could achieve goals, or had a lot of things that they wanted out of life, because they didn't feel they had enough time. Others felt that they didn't have enough money.

The crazy idealist

I began to think of different ideas that would remove these two factors so that people would be free to dream and think about the possibilities of what they could achieve in life. I was listening to a motivational program by Brian Tracy, and he spoke about his concept of the **Crazy Idealist**, a technique he uses when setting goals.

Suddenly something clicked. I now had a good idea of how I could remove the factors of time and money from being a barrier that stopped many people from setting goals. Picture this—we have just boarded a plane and the destination is Las Vegas, Nevada. Once we arrive we are going to take a limo and go to a special casino where everybody wins. You and I are no different, and in no time each of us has won five million dollars. With this kind of money the sky is the limit and you have nothing but time on your hands and money to enjoy all the things previously you could only have dreamed about. If you like to play golf, you could build a house on a golf course. If you like to travel you could fly to Spain for breakfast, Italy for lunch, and Paris for dinner.

With that in mind, take out your pad of paper, and at the top label it **Crazy Idealist.**

Begin to write down everything that you want to **Be, Do, and Have**. You don't want to stop writing until you have everything on this Crazy Idealist. List the people you want to meet, places you want to go, and things that you want to do. When you're completely finished, put this Crazy Idealist away for twenty-four hours so it has time to settle into your subconscious mind.

The next day pick up the **Crazy Idealist** and follow the same process as you did with the SMART goal setting method. I found that those individuals who use this formula easily remove some of the mental barriers that keep them from achieving their goals and also accelerate the process.

To access the Crazy Idealist forms go to: **www.DrRickGoodman. com/Imachampion**.

Storyboarding

Many individuals—from businessmen and women to professional athletes and movie studios—utilize a technique of goal setting called **storyboarding**. I learned this technique while watching the making of the Disney movie *The Lion King* on PBS, the educational network. Walt Disney had a process that he went through every time he crafted a movie or cartoon. He would have individual pieces of cardboard with individual scenes pasted on each one, depicting the action from one to the next. This way, everybody working together on a feature length film or cartoon has the same idea of what the scene should look and feel like.

This is just another way of instituting the habit of beginning with the end in mind. Whenever our senses are exposed to a thought, feeling, or idea, it becomes more real for us.

As Maxwell Maltz stated, **"The mind does not know the difference between something actually happening and something imagined vividly in great detail."**

Storyboarding is easy to do. It will encompass your vision for all that you want in the future. All you need is a piece of poster board or cardboard to get started. Even file folders will work. Cut larger pieces into smaller pieces (copy paper size will work). Then cut out pictures of the things that you want most, from magazines or from whatever source you can find, including the Internet. Paste one on each of the "boards,"and you now will have your own storyboard of goals and dreams. Arrange and rearrange them any way you want. It's your storyboard and you have complete control of it—and your life!

Sometimes I use my screensaver as my storyboard, placing pictures of places that I want to visit, famous vacation spots around the world, sporting events I want to attend, and people that I would like to meet. That way my goals are right there for me to see all the time. There are no right or wrong rules in this process. Just go with your feelings and dream big.

Getting your day off to a great start!

Great teams and Super Bowl champions (and individuals) begin their days on a positive note. How you start your day is going to have an enormous impact on achieving your goals and dreams.

Professional athletes practice (and practice and practice), and the first thing they do is warm up, stretching out their muscles, and preparing themselves for competition.

You and I are no different. We need to stretch out and warm up our mental muscles every day so we can achieve peak performance. I start my day the same way every single day. If you are sitting outside my bedroom you would hear me say three things:

(1) The first thing I always say to myself is, **"Every day above ground is a great day."** I figure if I wake up I'm ahead of the game. Some people did not wake up today and you can bet, for them, it's not such a great day. We hope it's no one we know. Set yourself up for success right from the start it makes a difference.

(2) The second thing I say, every single day is, **"What's going to happen today to make it a great day?"** I want my brain consistently searching for what's going to happen to make it a great day. I want to figure it out. Even if some things aren't going the way I want them to, I want to attract and focus on what's good in every situation.

Just the other day I woke up around 6 a.m. and said to myself, "What's going to happen today to make it a great day?" As I went throughout my day I continued to ask myself this question over and over. Around four o'clock I went to the dry cleaners to pick up some shirts and Mark, the owner, came over to me to say hello, and showed me what he had found. It was my favorite pair of pants I thought I had lost on the road in one of the many hotels I had stayed in when doing keynote speeches. These pants had been lost for a year, or so I thought. This certainly made it a great day for me. Think about what you want to attract in your life. Remember the stars shine brightest when the sky is darkest. It's easy to look for the bad things that happen in a day, but it is just as easy to look for the good!

(3) The third thing I say to myself is, **"How can I make it a great day and enjoy the process?"** I want to figure out how I can make it a great day and enjoy the process of going through it. Most people go from point A to point Z and don't get to enjoy the journey in between. I have heard many a motivational speaker say some variation of this—**"Success is a journey, not a destination."** Enjoying the process of success will make your victories much sweeter.

It's a great world out there with more opportunities than ever before for individuals who want everything out of life. When you have a game plan for success there will be no stopping you on your journey to "Living a Championship Life."

LIVING A CHAMPIONSHIP LIFE
ACTION STEP 2:

List Your Top Five Goals and Your Deadline for Accomplishing Them

1.

2.

3.

4.

5.

CHAPTER 3
CLOCK MANAGEMENT

Every great team and every great quarterback must learn how to manage the clock. The effect it has on the outcome of the game is critical. The 1999 St. Louis Rams' goal was to strike quickly and strike often, which put enormous strain on their opponent's offensive and defensive units.

Bill Belichick, the coach of the New England Patriots, has a different philosophy on clock management. His goal is to have long, sustained drives, keeping his offense on the field and wearing down the opponent's defense.

The 2008 Super Bowl champion New York Giants utilized the same philosophy as the New England Patriots have been using for years while building their dynasty in the NFL. The goal for the Giants was to pressure Tom Brady, New England's MVP quarterback, into making poor decisions by taking away the time he had to manage his offense.

Clock management in your personal and professional lives is no different than a football game. In order to be successful, and "live a championship life," you are going to have to manage your time as if your day is a sixty-minute game.

The good news is, with the technology that we have available to us today we are able to accomplish multiple tasks in a shorter period of time than ever before. In just the last five years I have been able to more than double the amount of work that I can get done in half the time it used to take. It's more important than ever before, with all the demands that take place in our lives for us to be able to manage our time and maximize our lives.

It's been my experience that individuals who implemented just one of these clock management techniques generally increased their effectiveness and productivity by twenty-five percent. Individuals who implemented two of these ideas noticed an increase of fifty percent in their productivity. The biggest jump in productivity happened to individuals who implemented at least three ideas. They noticed an increase in their productivity of over one hundred percent, saving them time and creating wealth.

The surprising news is, the majority of these techniques and systems require very little technical knowledge, and they can be implemented immediately. The following are a number of techniques, products, and systems that we use in our office that have assisted us in growing our business.

Years ago I sat in a lecture and the speaker talked about the three organizing components that would contribute to an A+ business. Since then I have implemented this philosophy in every aspect of my personal and professional lives, with outstanding results.

Three Components That Contribute to an A+ business

In order to grow your business and excel in the future, it's important that you understand the three components that contribute to an A+ office. The three components are **simplicity, speed, and efficiency.** Let's take a look at them individually and see how they work.

Simplicity. All of the systems you design for your business must be simple enough that you can replicate them and train any individuals on your team to step in and do the job. The area where most businesses fail in this respect is when only a limited number of individuals in the organization understand the process. At that point the process and system are basically held hostage. In business **knowledge is power only when it's shared**.

Let's look at the most basic example, a company everyone should know called McDonald's.

Tomorrow you can take your family to McDonald's in Miami, San Francisco, or St. Louis, and order french fries at each of these locations. What you will find is the french fries will always taste the same no matter the geographical location where they are purchased.

The reason behind this is simple—McDonald's has a process for making french fries. In fact, it's printed on one piece of paper so that all employees follow the same procedures. How's that for simplicity?

LIVING A CHAMPIONSHIP LIFE ACTION STEP 3:

Look at some of the basic systems in your office, the ones that have to do with communications, handling paperwork, and keeping in touch with your clients and prospective customers. When you do this, ask yourself the following question:

What can I do to simplify the existing systems that I already have in place in my business?

Once you have the answer to that question. It's time to take action on the system!

Speed. Today we live in a world that is getting flatter by the moment. In fact, in 1992 the Internet was rolled out as the World Wide Web. Within five years the Internet grew from 600,000 users to over forty million, doubling every fifty-three days. In order to grow your business well into the future, you must be able to deliver information to anyone, at any time, anywhere in the world in a matter of seconds.

In order to grow your business you're going to have to analyze your communications systems, your e-mail delivery systems, your phone system, and your written correspondence. People in the world today don't want to wait for anything, especially time-sensitive information. They want fast food, fast service and especially, fast information, and **the good news is they're willing to pay for it!**

LIVING A CHAMPIONSHIP LIFE ACTION STEP 4:

Analyze the systems that you use in your office and see what you can do about decreasing the turnaround time in which your business disseminates information. Once you are able to decrease the turnaround time of getting information in the hands of your clients and prospective customers, you will see an immediate increase in your business.

Efficiency. The last component that contributes to an A+ office is **efficiency.** The first impression that you make to a potential client or customer may be the only one that you get. Therefore you must be efficient in your process and eliminate mistakes. Statistics indicate that most repeat mistakes come from a lack of focus or inefficiency of the existing systems in place.

LIVING A CHAMPIONSHIP LIFE ACTION STEP 5:

Analyze all your systems in order to eliminate redundancy and increase the speed at which the systems operate.

Business Systems That Lead to Efficiency

In order to prepare your business and solidify your office infrastructure it is important to be able to count on key systems in your office. I have identified five areas that contribute to the efficiency of an office and enable the business to grow at an accelerated pace. The five areas that have the most impact on the business are the

Computer Systems, Data Entry Systems, Voicemail Systems, Communications Systems, Dictation and Correspondence Systems.

Let's break each one of these five areas down and address them individually.

Computer Systems. It is important that your office has a computer system that is easy to operate and is user friendly for all of your staff members, including yourself. I have found that a majority of the offices that have had problems in the past with their computer systems, experienced problems because only a limited number of individuals in the company had any experience with the existing system. The leader in most instances, delegated the training of the computer systems to everyone else but themselves. This has all the makings of a **Hostage Crisis!**

Let's look at this case scenario. One of your key people decide that he or she is going to leave on an extended vacation, and then never even comes back to your office. You are now held hostage by your own computer system. This has happened to me. I had to learn a whole computer system in one day out of desperation, not inspiration. It is my goal to save anyone who reads this book all of the stress that I felt when that incident happened. How much smarter would it have been to implement cross-training on the computer? Also, having a third party computer consultant on retainer would have reduced the problems and stress considerably.

SO MASTER ALL OF YOUR SYSTEMS!

There are a number of good computer systems and software packages on the market today. We recommend that our clients perform an Internet search in order to get the maximum amount of information on the systems that are out there today. Technology is changing daily—often hourly—and by searching the Internet you will likely find the most up-to-date information available.

The best way to find out the information you need is to go to the search engine **www.google.com** and enter your request in the search bar. Whether it's hardware or software, Google's search engine will provide you with the latest information on product availability. There are also a number of systems that will allow you to take a no-cost test drive of their software to see if it works for you and your organization.

Client contact management programs. In every professional sport, the general manager of the team is responsible for negotiating contracts and interacting with the sports agents who represent the athletes. The more details that an agent knows about the general managers—likes, dislikes, wants and needs—the easier it will be for them get acceptable contracts for their players to sign with the team.

Just like a good agent who has a highly detailed database, it's important that you have a contact information system that will help you to better communicate with your customers and the people that you come in contact with on a daily basis. A client contact management program will help you organize and grow your customer lists, which in turn, will help you to grow your business.

The program that we prefer is the **Act Program** for contact management. It's easy to use and simple to teach, and you can find it anywhere on the Web or at any of your local office or computer stores. The program will interface with your Blackberry, Microsoft Outlook, and many other programs, too.

Data Entry. Because of the constant flow of information and our increased need to compile data, we have looked for ways to handle it more efficiently, and at a lower cost. We have decided to model the business behavior of a majority of the Fortune 500 companies in the world. We have begun to send work overseas, to India, where they perform data entry and a multitude of other administrative tasks at a third of the price that it would cost us to do in the United States. This has drastically increased the efficiency and growth of our legal CLE business, Advantage Legal Seminars, **www.advantagelegalseminars.com**.

Some business owners may fear sending information to the other side of the world. However, after reading the book, *The World Is Flat,* by Thomas Friedman, we came to understand that India has vast resources of human potential that could help us to be more efficient in our own businesses in the United States.

The company in India that we recommend to our clients is a group called **Flatworld Solutions,** and the best way to get in touch with them and find out their menu of services is to go to **www.outsource2India.com.** The more efficient your record keeping and correspondence is, the more your business will be able to handle new customers.

Voicemail. People today have less time and even less patience than ever before. They want information right away and they want to get to the person they need immediately. There is no room in business anymore for a receptionist who just answers the phone. This position needs to be filled by somebody who is a grandmaster at multitasking administrative duties.

One area to **save money, become more efficient, and explode your business** is using a **virtual answering service.** They utilize a professional voice person who's used in commercials on radio and television. You get to write your own message which you can use to help market your business, while guaranteeing the consistent quality of the message that your clients get.

With many of the companies out there, you can get a 888, 866, or 877 extension at a fraction of the cost that it would be to go directly through your local phone company. The system that we use routes calls directly to the people who can best help our customers. The one company that we recommend for our clients is **www.VirtualPBX.com.** The starting cost for this system is around $9.99 a month, plus a minimal fee for incoming calls.

Communication Systems. Businesses grow or fail based on their internal communication with their staff and their external communication with their clients. As the world gets flatter you want to use systems that will increase communication speed without increasing overhead. The quickest and most cost-effective way to communicate today is through **e-mail.** Thousands of businesses use this as their primary communication tool.

Recently we performed a survey of what our customers around the world thought of e-mail today. They felt that it was both impersonal and over-utilized in its present form. However, with today's technology, we can enhance the process. There are two new ways of communicating that we have been recommending to our clients in order to improve the delivery of information.

We recommend that you get a program called **Skype.** You can find it at **www.Skype.com.** Skype is a voice-operated Internet provider. Best of all, it's **Free!** Just go to Skype.com and download the program. All you need is a set of headphones with a microphone attached, and you're up and running. Here's the great news! If any of your clients or friends do the same thing and they have Skype, you can call them anywhere in the world for **Free.** Who says nothing in this world is free?

Most of our clients have taken this process one step further. They have purchased a web cam made by a company called Logitech. It's called the **Logitech Fusion Web Cam,** and it costs around $39. You can get it at Best Buy, OfficeMax, or any computer store. The simplest way to get it is to go to their website at **www.Logitech.com.**

When you combine the web cam with your e-mail or Skype phone, you can **send video messages** to your clients and **conduct live web conferences** anywhere in the world. If that doesn't help you grow your business I don't know what will! The company that we recommend with the best e-mail and marketing program out there is a company called **Indivo.** You can reach them at 954-919-7000. Just ask for Corey or visit them on the web at **www.indivo.com.** They will be more than happy to set you up with an e-mail marketing program that will fit your budget and explain to you the other services that **Indivo** has to offer.

Dictation and Correspondence. The ability to correspond quickly with words and writing give you the ability to grow your business. Some of you are just like me and have a major administrative weakness. I'm talking about the inability to type quickly. I think my maximum speed when fully concentrating is about fifteen words per minute. That was until I discovered a great software program that eliminates my weaknesses altogether.

The program is called **Dragon Naturally Speaking 9.0 preferred.** It is a voice recognition software program. I can speak into my computer and the program does the typing for me, up to one hundred and sixty words per minute. Just the other day I was able to write nine articles in an hour and a half. It only takes about ten minutes to train on the whole system. The really cool thing that the program does is it scans all your existing documents and uploads words that are commonly used in your correspondence.

Once it is done scanning it adds those words to its already existing three hundred and fifty thousand word vocabulary that is built into the program. Again, you can find this program at any one of those local computer stores.

The next piece of technology that we suggest our clients get is a **Digital Voice Recorder.** The one that we recommend to our clients is the **Olympus WS 320M.** I got mine from **www. Amazon.com** for a little over one hundred dollars. Since then the prices have dropped drastically. The digital recorder is no bigger than a small lighter and can record up to thirty-six hours of information.

The way we use this device to enhance our communication and maximize our efficiency is to bring it to all of our meetings and seminars. recording everything that happens. When I am done recording, I hit a little button on the back of the digital recorder, which reveals a USB plug. I then upload the recorder and it's contents to my computer and run the recording of that meeting or seminar through the **Dragon System** which then gives me transcripts of everything that we've recorded.

Just think about how much time that will save you and how much more information you will be able to capture. This simple piece of technology will save you money and time while making you more efficient. With the digital tape recorder, you will never miss or forget that **Million Dollar Idea** again!

Clock Management: Your Daily Weekly and Monthly Schedule

Every NFL team has a **playbook** that represents the goals and objectives of what the offense, defense, and special teams are attempting to accomplish. The playbook has hundreds of plays and different scenarios of how the game might play out.

The teams that have won the Super Bowl understand what it takes to win the big game. They make adjustments at halftime to keep themselves moving in the right direction, eventually attaining their ultimate objective which is to become the Super Bowl champions.

Your daily, weekly, and monthly schedules are no different than a team playbook in the National Football League or any other sport. The schedule—just like the playbook—becomes your plan of attack for accomplishing all your goals and objectives. It's important that you take time to plan your weekly schedule around the activities that can give you the most return on your time investment.

On Saturday mornings before the game, most professional football teams perform a ritual known as the **walk-through**. It usually takes place at the team's training facility or in a hotel ballroom where the team is staying. The players actually walk through the exact plays that they intend to run the next day. This process of reviewing the playbook and performing a dress rehearsal of what they want to happen is essential to team success.

In order to increase your chances of success in maximizing your time and increasing your productivity, it's important that you continually **review and adjust your schedule** to meet your daily, weekly, and monthly obligations. As I stated earlier, I believe it's important to review your goals. Three times a day. You should also do the same thing with your daily and weekly schedule, which should also include your "**To-Do List.**"

Many times people remember the last thing they hear and read before they go to sleep, and they remember the first thing they hear and read in the morning. How many times have you listened to a song on the radio or read something before you went to sleep that you just couldn't get out of your head? Maybe it was the last song you heard on the radio before you went to work, or heard on the way to work, and you sang it all day long. It might have been a horrible song, but you couldn't get it out of your head.

The information that most of us review before we go to sleep, and the things that we listen to first thing in the morning, tend to stay with us all day long.

Just like the effectiveness of the Saturday walk-through in helping a team achieve victory, it's important for you to do a **mental walk-through** daily (or even more frequently) of your "To-Do List." This way you can increase your chances of accomplishing all your goals and objectives in a fixed amount of time.

Why Use a To-Do List. Many people ask me why I still continue to use a hand-written to-do list. And I reply that it works for me. Remember there are no hard and fast rules regarding the format or technique that you use when making a to-do list. You might prefer Day-Timers, or the list feature on your computer. I have found that the best techniques are the ones that we feel most comfortable implementing. But it's important, as Nike says, to "Just Do It."

There are many benefits in keeping an organized to-do list other than the obvious increase in productivity you will notice in your personal and professional lives. For example:

- It keeps all necessary tasks from slipping through the cracks

- It ensures new innovative tasks will be considered

- It facilitates accurate prioritization of all tasks

- It allows you to consider constantly emerging tasks

- Having all projects and tasks listed in one place helps to reduce the feeling of being overwhelmed.

Today most people's lives are busier than ever before, with work, family, and many other obligations taking up our time. It's easy for tasks, applications, and opportunities to slip through the cracks. By keeping a focused to-do list, and reviewing it daily, your chances of success will be greatly increased.

The Magic Notepad. How many times have you had a one million dollar idea in the middle of the night, but couldn't remember what it was in the morning? I know, if you're like me, this has happened to you hundreds of times and you probably have lost thousands, if not millions, of dollars of potential income. It doesn't have to happen like that anymore.

What you need is a **Magic Notepad**! Now it's not really a magic notepad. It could be any type of pad of paper, a legal pad, a journal, a pocket notebook, or just a scratch piece of paper. The reason why I call it the magic notepad is because excellent ideas come to you when your mind is relaxed. If you have a way of writing or recording this information down when it first hits you, it may just be the best idea you ever have.

Just recently I woke up in the middle of the night and an idea hit me. I just signed a contract to do a keynote speech for a major health organization at their annual meeting. The theme of the program was "Striving for Excellence," and it was important for me to be able to customize a program that would match this client's needs.

Sometime around 2:30 a.m. I woke up, and started to write. The entire speech just popped into my head. I called the presentation **"Striving for Excellence: What We Do and the People We Touch."** I started to see the program from the perspective of the people who worked in this organization, whether they were involved in management or were front-line employees, and how they had a positive impact on the clients of the practice and their fellow workers.

Sometimes the best ideas come to us while we're working out in the gym or relaxing in the backyard. The most important thing you can do to **capture these million-dollar moments** is to make sure that you always have a method of writing and recording information, whether you are at home, in your office, in your car—anywhere!

Clock Management: Prioritizing Your Work. How do you prioritize your work? Some people might say that they work on the easiest things first, the things they love to do. Other people might choose the hardest tasks to do, just to get them out of the way. If you want to get ahead and live a championship life, it's important that you are working on the tasks that have the most benefit to you and your organization.

Some people ask me how I determine what tasks are the highest priorities when I'm working with different organizations. The answer to that is pretty simple. I just ask! On many occasions the people in charge of the project assume that I already have the answers and understand the priorities of the organization when I really don't. Has this ever happened to you? The simple task of asking not only shows that you're interested in the task, but will also help to clarify the priorities.

Another way of prioritizing tasks and responsibilities is by using Stephen Covey's quadrant system of urgent verse important tasks. In an effort to simplify the system that Covey described in his bestseller *Seven Habits of Highly Effective People*, I have renamed some of the quadrants for my own use when prioritizing tasks and responsibilities. This chart enables me to simplify the act of prioritization based on the amount of time I have and its impact on my organization's bottom-line.

To view the Living a Championship Life priority quadrant go to: **www.DrRickGoodman.com/Imachampion**

Quadrant #1: Dealing with Crisis, also known as "Putting out Fires."

Over the last ten years I've interviewed managers, supervisors, and CEOs of major corporations, who were constantly in crisis mode. In fact, some of these individuals were spending ninety percent of their time just dealing with problems and putting out fires, both in their personal and professional lives. In actuality, this should only take up about ten percent of your time.

Quadrant #2: Meetings, Goals, and Long-Range Planning

This quadrant represents all your meetings, goals, and long-range planning. This area should comprise approximately sixty-five percent of your time. The more time you spend in quadrant two the less time you will end up in quadrant one, in crisis mode. The importance of goals, long-range planning, and the sharing of information cannot be underestimated if you want to achieve balance in your personal and professional lives.

If you truly want to Live a Championship Life, everybody on your team—from your coworkers to your customers—have to be on the same page and receiving the same message, or your chances of succeeding will be diminished.

Quadrant two can have a great effect on your ability to achieve balance in your personal life as well. It's important to schedule time to spend with your family and friends. They are your ultimate support system. It's even more important to share your goals with the people that you truly love and who truly love you.

It is my firm belief that your support system is your lifeline to success!

You may have heard people say that the journey to success can be a long, hard, and bumpy road. I'm here to share with you some of my personal experiences. When we share the journey with the ones that we love, that hard and bumpy road will turn into a much smoother path, enabling you to enjoy a glorious ride through life, filled with defining moments and success beyond your wildest dreams.

From time to time, as most people have already experienced, life throws you a curve ball, and a guy named Murphy shows up. You probably know who I am talking about—Murphy, the guy with the law. As Murphy's Law says, "Whatever can go wrong will go wrong." Living on planet Earth makes it inevitable that we will end up in crisis at some point in our lives. As long as we focus on our quadrant number two activities, we should be able to minimize this effect.

Quadrant #3: Group activities

Quadrant three is labeled **group activities**. What are group activities? Group activities can include returning phone calls, answering e-mails, picking up the kids from school or extracurricular activities, even going to the grocery store or the dry cleaners. These are activities you can simply **group together** in order to be more efficient. Here's a perfect, personal example:

Recently I was in St. Louis visiting my children and my friends. I decided I was going to barbecue for everybody at my friend Richie's house that night for dinner. I went to the local grocery store to pick up some of St. Louis's finest ribs. The trip to the grocery store took about forty-five minutes. I walked into the house, and unpacked the food. I then went outside to fire up the grill. You probably have anticipated what happened next!

There was no gas in the barbecue grill! Has this ever happened to you? So I got back into my car, and drove over to the local Home Depot to exchange the empty tank. By the time I returned to the house another thirty minutes had passed and everyone was getting hungry. I hooked up the tank, turned on the barbecue grill and called out to my friend Rich, who was inside the house.

I asked him to bring me the KC Masterpiece barbecue sauce that was in the cabinet. If you love St. Louis barbecue like I do, you know there's only one barbecue sauce to use, and that's KC Masterpiece. I had just bought a full bottle of KC Masterpiece a week before when I was in town to see my son's baseball game, so I knew it would still be there. After a pause, Richie yelled back to me to say that all the barbecue sauce was gone, that he had used it up only a couple of days ago.

You know what happened next. I got back in my car and drove over to the local grocery store, which took another thirty minutes, and picked up a new bottle of KC Masterpiece barbecue sauce.

Has this ever happened to you? It took me over two hours to get a simple barbecue going and that doesn't include the time it took to cook the ribs.

When you are able to group your activities together and address them at certain times of the day, your day will become more efficient. This is known as **Block Scheduling**.

For example here are some ideas for implementing block scheduling. You can:

• Answer your e-mails at set times each day

• Return phone calls at preplanned times

• Group your meetings back to back at set times throughout the day

• Make a list of everything that you need at the grocery store so you won't have to make more than one trip

Quadrant #4: Junk

This is your final quadrant, and I call it **Junk**! This should comprise about five percent of your day. This is the unavoidable stuff, the little things that come across your desk in the day that will have little to no impact on the outcome of your goals and objectives, and there is not much you can do about them.

When you utilize the quadrant system in order to manage your time, you will accomplish more of your goals and objectives with less stress and more balance in your life.

There is another element that affects clock management, and that's called **Cycle Time**. Some people are morning people, others are afternoon people, still others are night owls. Statistics indicate that whether you believe you are a morning person or you think you are an afternoon person, most people are most productive the first two hours of the day. This is the time of day when you should be focusing on your quadrant one and quadrant two activities. You need to have the most focus when you're operating in crisis mode and putting out the fires that you experience at work or at home.

It's also important to be on your game when you're in your meetings to discuss your goals and objectives or involved in strategic planning sessions for your organization. In the last few years there have been a number of players in the National Football League who have been fined for being late to team meetings, missing them entirely, and even falling asleep in team meetings. In fact, some players have not only been fined but have also been asked to stay home and sit out the Super Bowl game because of their lack of respect for the importance of the team meetings and its ultimate effect on the chemistry of the team.

The good news is, you can change your cycle time with just a little discipline and planning. Think about this, how often have you had an appointment, when you knew you had to be somewhere at a certain time? Let's say you are what we would call an afternoon person, but today, you have an early morning meeting at 8:30 a.m., and you know that in order to arrive on time you must wake up by 6:30 a.m.

Did you wake up before your alarm clock went off?

It's been my experience that people who have important agenda items on their brain and know that they have to wake up at a certain time, are able to do it nine times out of ten. Suddenly they find the amazing ability to change their cycle time and wake up before the alarm clock goes off.

Maybe you remember as a kid right after summer vacation was over and it was time to go back to school. It was probably difficult to wake up for that first week of school, However, once you got into the second and third weeks of school you again started to wake up before that alarm clock went off.

This was no miracle; it was just an example of conditioning. When you condition your mind and your body to work in the cycle times that are most directly related to your lifestyle, both personally and professionally, you will be able to master anything that comes your way.

Clock Management: Capturing Your Time

If I could show you a simple method of how you can capture a minimum of twenty hours a week of lost time, would you be interested? Would you be willing to spend one week to find out where your time is going? Many people that I meet are interested in saving time, but they're not willing to invest the time necessary to find out where they're losing their time every single day!

Have you ever gone through a whole day and felt like you got nothing accomplished? Maybe you have even said to yourself, "This was the biggest waste of a day and wasted time that I've had in a long time." (If you say this every day, you're really in trouble!) If someone asked you what you did that day you probably wouldn't even be able to tell them and it's likely that day would be one big blur.

The Time Log

There is a technique that I have been using for the last twenty years. Although it may be antiquated in this day of technology, I find that keeping a **Time Log** has given me the ability to save countless hours of lost time, manage my personal and professional lives better, and to communicate more effectively with my employees.

Over the years I have heard many objections from audience members to keeping a time log. Some of them believe that they already know how they spend their day. Others feel that they just don't have enough time to invest in assessing their situation. These are nothing but lame excuses which demonstrate failure to recognize the problem and solution.

It's been my experience that we all lose time, minute by minute. Remember the example of my St. Louis barbecue where I had to make three trips to get a meal started? In that one instance alone, I lost an hour and a half of my time by not being prepared.

Just think about all the times when you've been interrupted. Maybe you were in that mental zone—you know, the one when you're getting massive amounts of work accomplished—when someone comes in and interrupts you, and you can't get back to that mental spot again. We've all been there!

So here is a concept that I've been using for years. I call it "**The Price-Value Ratio.**" This means if it's worth an hour of your time to invest in order to save you hours on end in the future, then do it. If not, then don't do it!

How often should you complete a time log? The answer is, for one week, five days every fiscal quarter, if you want to assess how your time is spent at work, and seven days if you're looking to include your weekends. Here are some techniques for keeping a time log:

- Record each transition from one task to another.

- Be specific. The more specific your timeline is regarding events and projects the more efficient and effective it will be.

- Abbreviate. Don't write a book. Keep it simple. For instance, if you're going to use names, use abbreviations that work for you. Examples: Debbie Smith-DS; Questions-Q; outgoing calls-OC; incoming calls-IC. Use whatever makes sense to you; this is for your eyes only. Developing your personal shorthand saves time and space.

- Record throughout the day. Note the time, activity, purpose, and priority (high, medium or low priority). This is your call! Here is an example of a time log:

TIME	EVENT	PURPOSE	PRIORITY
8:00 AM-8:10	TJIC	Tom Jones incoming call to discuss the game on Sun.	Low
8:15-8:30	DSV	Debbie Smith drop in visit to ask me a question regarding the quarterly report	Med
8:30-8:50	RGOC	Rick Goodman outgoing call to client	High
8:50-9:20	DSV	Debbie Smith just dropped in to ask me the same question she asked me 20 minutes ago	Low

Let's take a look at this example of a time log for evaluation and clock management purposes. This will help us to evaluate how our time is being spent and also help to educate those people in our office who are robbing us of our time.

Time Log Summary. From 8 a.m. to 8:10 a.m. the notation in the time log is **TJIC**. Tom Jones **Incoming Call**, the purpose was to discuss Sunday's football game. Now in the scheme of things I love to talk about football however on a Monday morning at eight o'clock this is not a very high priority.

From 8:15 a.m. to 8:30 a.m. the notation in the time log is **DSV**. Debbie Smith **Drop in Visit**. The purpose was to ask me a question regarding the quarterly report. This is a pretty important issue and needs to be handled properly. I spent fifteen minutes covering her question and when she left the office she seemed to understand what needed to be done.

From 8:30 a.m. to 8:50 a.m. the notation in the time log is **RGOC**. Rick Goodman **Outgoing Call**. The purpose was to call a client regarding a contract, and the priority was high.

From 8:50 a.m. to 9:20 a.m. the notation in the time log is **DSV**. Debbie Smith just dropped in to ask me the same question she asked me twenty minutes ago. Now the priority for this event was low.

If you're like me, when you get to work on Monday morning, the first thing that you want to do is to get organized for the rest of the week. When I sat down to record my time log I noticed in just the first hour and twenty minutes of my day I spent thirty-five minutes of my time answering the same questions from the same employee twice.

Now I know Debbie Smith did not wake up on a Monday morning and say to herself, how can I ask my employer the same question over and over again, and drive him crazy? That's just not how people think. She may not even recognize how many times that she has dropped into my office or how much of my time she has taken. This is the beauty of the time log. You now get to play a game that you learned in kindergarten called **Show and Tell**. I have found that when I sit down with an employee and share with them my time log I am able to correct a lot of communication issues, and also protect my time.

If I was going to script my communication with Debbie in order to assure the best outcome, it would go something like this:

"Debbie, I have been keeping a time log of the events that take place in my office and I noticed on my log that you dropped in to my office a number of times in order to clarify information and ask me some very important questions.

"I just want you to know that my goal is to see you be successful in everything that you do in our organization and if I can do anything to help that's what I'm going to do. So what I'd like to do is set a time between 2 and 2:30 p.m. today to cover any questions that you might have regarding the quarterly reports.

"Could you also do me a favor and save up all the questions that you have and write everything down on an agenda so that we can go over it together in our meeting? Is that fair?"

I do like to ask the question, "Is that fair?" I find this very effective, since I already know the answer. Of course it's fair. Remember my goal is to help them and to answer their questions.

Let's analyze some of the benefits of the show-and-tell technique. Debbie is now aware that she has dropped in on me a number of times this morning alone. She also understands how much I value her as an employee and that my goal is to see her be successful in our organization.

At the same time, she has received a subliminal message that is asking her in a positive way to save all of her questions for our meeting in the afternoon.

This technique has helped me to build relationships, communicate more effectively, and to save hours on end in the long run. I know it will do the same for you. If you feel as strongly as I do about capturing your time in order to improve your productivity. You can access the time log at:

www.drrickgoodman.com/Imachampion

LIVING A CHAMPIONSHIP LIFE
ACTION STEP 6:

By this point, you should have a number of different systems and techniques that should help you to better manage your time, maximize your efficiency, and increase your productivity. Pick any three systems, techniques or product recommendations and implement them for thirty days. You will be amazed at how easy it is to accomplish your goals and objectives when you are totally organized.

There has never been a team in the history of the National Football League or any other team sport that has won a championship without managing the clock. I know that when you manage your own clock, you'll be on your way to living a championship life!

CHAPTER 4
COMMUNICATION MASTERY

Throughout the history of the Super Bowl there have been a number of great coaches. Names like Vince Lombardi, Tom Landry, Bill Walsh, Bill Parcells, Dick Vermeil, and Bill Belichick. Each one of these coaches had their strengths and weaknesses, utilizing different motivational techniques to attain their ultimate goal, which was to win the Super Bowl.

There was one common thread that each one of these famous coaches shared—they were all master communicators. Communicating clearly to your boss, employers, coworkers, friends, children, spouse or significant other, is a critical part of your success and is directly related to your ability to improve your conditions in your personal and professional lives. Many people are of the belief that master communicators are born, not made, and that some people are just naturally good at public speaking and motivating others. This couldn't be further from the truth. Communications skills are like any other skills that can be learned and mastered, until they become a habit.

Master communicators understand that life is about dealing with many different types of people. They're the ones to whom we have to answer, such as our boss or employer; the people who are around us, particularly our friends and colleagues; and the people who look up to us—who we hope are our family, children, and employees.

Master communicators know how to make contact with each one of these groups, and understand that by helping them to achieve their goals, they will ultimately help themselves to achieve their own goals and objectives. It just goes to say, if you can't communicate with other people, you will dramatically decrease your chances for success in your personal and professional lives.

How well a coach communicates with his players during a big game is no different than how you must communicate on a day-to-day basis in order to be successful in your business. When there is a breakdown in communication in the big game, it often results in a turnover, whether it's a fumble, an interception, or just a loss of downs and yardage. The breakdown of communication is usually the root cause. It's amazing to me how many managers don't communicate their personal goals and/or their company's goals. Invariably this failure to communicate their goals to the rest of the organization ends up creating more problems for managers in the long run.

Establishing Rapport

Effective communication can be one of the best problem solvers in the world, but so many of us don't know how to go about it properly. We talk and talk yet we don't communicate. We don't establish that personal connection that is so important in order to get our message across. I have always lived by the philosophy that; **"People do business with people who they like, who are like them."**

This really means that if people like you for who you are as an individual, you will have a better opportunity of getting your message across.

That's why it's imperative that you **establish rapport** with all the people who you communicate with on a regular basis, at work and at home. The easiest way to build rapport with any individual is to simply find something that you have in common with them. It could be anything—people you both know, places you've been, movies or concerts that you've seen, great books that you've read, or even talking about your children—can all be great icebreakers. This can open the door for you to establish rapport with whomever you're communicating at the time. My years of research on communicating and building rapport with people have taught me that there are different kinds of communicating, depending on to whom I am talking.

I've been giving motivational speeches to companies around the world for the last twenty years. When I am speaking to large groups my goal is to create an air of enthusiasm or a buzz in the crowd. The communication style that I use with this type of group is one of high energy and passion so I can get my message across to a large number of people.

On the other hand, when I am communicating with one person, my style is completely different. A one-on-one conversation requires listening, never taking your eyes off the person, conveying the impression that the conversation is very important to you. It's talking in a relaxed, soothing tone because your goal is to have a **dialogue** with the person—to listen, to build trust, and to establish a relationship.

It's no different when you're speaking on the telephone. It's about building trust with someone far away. A common tip for speaking on the telephone is to "talk with a smile in your voice." And while you're talking to someone on the telephone, don't check your e-mails, cover the mouthpiece to talk to someone else, or—worst of all—eating and making chewing noises. All of these—and anything else which distracts you—are incredible turn-offs when you're communicating with someone.

I remember watching an interview on the news, and the star they were talking to was commenting about her visit to the Oprah Winfrey Show when she was promoting her autobiography. She went on and on and raved about what a great job Oprah did on the show that day. This really caught my attention. I was curious about why she thought Oprah did such a great job. The interviewer then asked the star an interesting question:

"Was there anything that Oprah did to make you feel that this was a great interview?"

The answer made me really stop and think. She said that when she sat down with Oprah and Oprah started to ask her questions about her life and her career, she felt like she was the only person in the room. It was "that laser beam focus" that Opera had in the interview that made the star feel so important. Based on this the star felt that it was one of the best interviews she ever had in her life.

President Time Consciousness

If you want to master communication, every conversation that you have with an individual one-on-one should be handled with P.T.C.—**Present Time Consciousness**. When the person that you're communicating with gets the feeling that they are the most important person in room you'll be able to build rapport with ease and efficiency. Making eye contact—and holding it very long—is difficult for many people. But be assured that good eye contact is a vital factor in building good rapport with other people.

If you still feel that it's difficult for you to build rapport with other people, here are some tips to use as icebreakers in order to start a conversation. Establish rapport by asking questions that:

• Appeal to their interests
• Prompt them to discuss their hobbies
• Complement them in some honest way
• Relate to the immediate scene (mounted fish on wall, hunting photo, trophy, etc.)

Now, I'm not saying it's going to be easy the first time that you start to consciously focus on building rapport and breaking the ice with people. But as I indicated earlier, communication is a habit and the more you practice the better you're going to get.

There are also some things that you probably should avoid when attempting to build rapport. Don't ask questions that:

- Are directly related to their personal lives (unless they bring them up, of course). These types of questions can make people feel uncomfortable. Some of the people might even resent the fact that you're asking them questions that pertain to their personal lives.
- Are controversial, and which might be opposite of their belief systems. The advice to "Avoid questions involving politics, health, and religion" is true most of the time.

The Kobe/Shaq factor

Often it's important to build rapport with people, even if you have nothing in common with them, especially if you're working on a team project or trying to achieve a common goal. Since I live in South Florida I've been lucky enough to be able to watch Shaquille O'Neal and Dwayne Wade score points every night for the Miami Heat, giving them their first NBA championship. These two players were able to build rapport on and off the basketball court.

The reason why Shaquille O'Neal ended up in Miami was partly due to the fact that the long-term relationship between him and Kobe Bryant—his former teammate with the Los Angeles Lakers—had disintegrated. One reason was that neither one of them had ever socialized with the other off the court. They really didn't have a lot in common, especially with the difference in their ages. The fact that they did not talk off the court or socialize had little bearing on their business relationship.

On the court was a completely different story. From the year 2000 until 2002 the Los Angeles Lakers won three NBA titles and dominated most of the teams that they played. After their third championship in a row, both of these players let their personal feelings get in the way of their business relationship. They were finally eliminated from the playoffs two years in a row and Shaquille O'Neal got the trade that he wanted out of Los Angeles and down to Miami. Since then, Shaq was traded to Phoenix, meaning he had to start all over again to try to build rapport and relationships.

In order to foster friendly feelings toward yourself—even when you have very little in common with the people on your team—it's important to understand a few basics. You need to believe that others like you and want to know you. Other people will pick up on your positive attitude and will be more likely to respond in a similar fashion.

Your positive attitude will influence others in a positive way. The opposite is also true—when you are negative you influence others in a negative way.

Let go of **F.E.A.R.—False Evidence Appearing Real.** When you have confidence, you will not have fear. Fear comes about when you're unsure of yourself. Make up your mind that you will show confidence in everything you do, even if on the inside you're a little unsure of your situation. Some of the most fascinating shots on television during highly competitive games, are those close-ups showing the intensity on the faces of individual players. People often remark on the face and eyes of Chicago Bears linebacker great, Mike Singletary. That look alone would freeze any opposing player. That was confidence!

Take a chance. One thing is certain, if you don't take a chance you'll miss the opportunity to break the ice and perhaps form a lasting relationship.

A.S.K.—IF YOU DON'T A.S.K., YOU WON'T G.E.T.

For years this was my credo. I look at it this way—what's the worst thing that can happen? If the person says yes to your request, you have just moved to the next level. If they say no, well, then you're just in the same spot as you were three minutes earlier. What do you have to lose? Ask!

I have seen dozens of times when friends of mine have walked up to a beautiful woman, who they thought was unapproachable, and asked them to dance, have a drink, etc. To the men's surprise, the women would say yes ninety percent of the time. Later on in the evening we would find out that most of these women were just hoping someone would come and ask them to dance. The fact of the matter is the first person who did ASK received the answer they were looking for. Unfortunately, most of us will never know what could have been because we didn't take that first step and A.S.K.!

• **Don't be overeager**. Just relax and be yourself. While fear and lack of confidence will not help you, neither does overconfidence. Just relax, be positive, and make the first move. In other words, just try to be you. That's the best thing you can do.

• **Smile**. This is your million-dollar asset. Smile naturally as you approach the other person. Your smile is going to be the first step expressing positive body language. When this happens the other person is more likely to respond in kind. Your body language is going to play a vital role in your communication skills.

Have you ever spoken to someone on the telephone and you could tell that they were either eating, not paying attention, or just doing something other than fully listening to you with present time consciousness? You could feel this right through the phone even though you may have been miles away. This has always been a big turnoff to me, and I assume it has been to you, too. The subliminal message that you're getting from the person that you're communicating with on the telephone is:

• You are not important!
• What you're saying doesn't matter!
• I've got more important things to do than listen to you!

When you communicate one-on-one with an individual, they are going to pick up on your body language more rapidly, so it's important that your thoughts, feelings, beliefs and your body, are in line with how you want to communicate with others.

Use Mirroring or Modeling Techniques

The science of neuro-linguistic programming utilizes **Mirroring or Modeling** techniques in a very powerful way. When you start a conversation, be aware of the other person's body language and copy it. If they stand up, you stand up; if they offer their hand, take it. Use the mirroring technique, but subtly. I have done this thousands of times in order to build rapport with patients of mine. The one thing that they would always say about me was, "I like him because he's just like me." By mirroring their behaviors they will feel that they have something in common with you. They may not be able to put their finger on it. It's just a feeling!

Years ago when I was just starting to study success, I used this technique a number of times with my ex-wife, Laurie. Example: I knew after a long week of seeing patients I wanted to go play a quick round of golf at our country club on the weekend. Having small children at the time made this difficult. So when I would get home from the office, I had to prepare myself mentally, in order to discuss with her the possibility of me playing nine holes of golf later that afternoon or eighteen the next morning. I remember the scene like it was yesterday.

I walked into the house and Laurie was sitting on the couch. I asked her how her day went and she started to talk to me about all the things that were going on in her life. I listened intently, remembering my lessons of present time consciousness. I then noticed that she crossed her right leg over her left leg and I did the same thing. When she was making a point she put her hand up on her chin. And I did the same thing. She nodded her head up and down as if to agree with what she was talking about, and I nodded my head up and down in the same manner, as if in agreement. She then looked at me and said, "I'm really glad that you understand what I'm talking about and how I am feeling."

I was now ready to go in for the kill! I looked directly at her and said, "Honey, would you mind if I go play eighteen holes of golf tomorrow morning with my buddies. I would really appreciate it, and we'll make sure to be back by noon." Her response was—in my mind what every male golfer on this planet would consider music to their ears—"No problem! Go have a great time and can you call me on the way home in case I may need you to pick something up from the grocery store!" Wow. It worked!

What I didn't tell you is that when I had mentioned to her earlier in the day about playing golf, her feelings were strongly aligned against it and she let me know that in no uncertain terms. I guess the moral of the story is that if you need to go out and play golf, or just do something on your own, and your spouse or significant other is not on the same page as you, implement some mirroring and modeling techniques and you just might get the response that you're looking for. Isn't it worth a try?

Communicate your goals, explain your needs

It's important to understand that a majority of motivation is connected directly to your dedication. Let me give you an example. Let's say I am on the phone at home and my two children are in the room. Here's the conversation:

"Alex, can you go out to the pool and put the skimmer and hose away and shut off the waterfall?" "Why me?" he says. "Why can't Jamie get it?" "Why can't Alex do it?" says Jamie. "Dad, I did it the last time," says Alex.

They both feel as if they've been picked on. This happens in the workplace all the time. The person in charge tells someone to do something, and his or her first reaction is, "Why me? How come they're always picking on me?" This is human nature. So now both of my children have complained about being asked to take care of the pool. Now it's back to Alex, the older one.

"Why me?" he asks. I tell him, "Because you understand where everything goes and how to operate the waterfalls. Plus you're the oldest, and you're much stronger than your sister." This makes all the difference in the world. He now has an understanding of why I want him to complete the task and he also understands why he is the right person to do it. He knows this was not done out of punishment, but out of awareness of his strengths and abilities. By taking a few seconds to explain to him the reason why he is being asked to do this, he now feels totally different about being asked to perform the task. I've spent the time to communicate with him instead of ordering him to do it.

I'm a bit of a rebel and my son has that independent streak in him also, which goes to say we don't want anybody to tell us what to do. I know there's a lot of other people in the world who feel exactly the same way as we do. When someone *asks* us for help we are much more apt to say yes than when someone *tells* us what to do.

Years ago, during the time of Henry Ford, the pioneer auto maker, when workers were told to do something, they simply complied. In today's day and age of technology, people are more informed and information is at your fingertips in seconds. People want to know why they're being asked to do something.

It's simply not enough to say "Because I told you so." The "I told you so" is an instant turnoff to most people, possibly the biggest one there is. Whether you are a parent, teacher, coach, employer, or whatever you may be, it's important to communicate your needs, and the why. Certainly there are going to be times when it's unavoidable to give orders. However, the small amount of time it takes to explain things will usually pay the biggest dividends.

Remember the price-value ratio we spoke about earlier. If it's worth your time to invest in—and it can save you money and time in the long run—then just do it. It's as simple as that!

Check Back: Your Key to Delegation Success

In order to grow your business, you're going to have to trust that your staff members are capable of getting the jobs done that you assign to them. That means you're going to have to do something that may be uncomfortable for some of you and easy for others. You're going to have to **delegate tasks** in order to grow your business. After all, you're only one person. You can't do it all.

What you are going to find is that some of your staff members can do certain jobs even better than you can, and by utilizing effective delegation techniques you will increase the odds of rapidly meeting your goals and objectives.

One of the best delegation techniques I've ever come across is one that I call **Check Back!**

Now check back is not check up. After all, if you're checking up on a staff member the first thought that comes into their mind is that you don't trust them. You could be the best worker on the planet and if somebody is standing behind your back, watching you do your job, you're going to make mistakes. So we use a technique called **Check Back**. Here's how it works:

Step One: **ASK.** When you assign a team member a task to do, ask them the question, "**When can I Check Back with you?**" The ball is now in their court. They have to give you a time when they are going to have the task completed and a commitment to getting it done. Now get out of the way!

Step Two: CHECK BACK. You Must Check Back! If you assign a task to a staff member and don't follow up at the assigned time, you're sending a message that you don't care. The next time you assign a task to that team member, they will drag their feet and be more likely to sabotage the process, or at least miss the deadline.

Step Three: SHOW APPRECIATION. If you have Checked Back with that employee and they've completed the task, **let them know how much you appreciate it**. If they have not completed the task, then you want to ask another key question. Example: you asked your children to go upstairs and clean up their room. You go upstairs an hour later and the room is not cleaned up. The first question that you ask your child is: "**Why?**" And the answer better not be, "**Because.**"

When we assign tasks to our employees, we expect them to complete the tasks, especially if they've made a commitment. Now if they don't like the task they are doing, that's okay. However we still expect them to see it through to the end. The next time a similar task comes up, we explain to them that they really don't have to do it. However, we explain to them the consequences, and then it's their choice. Taking away privileges seems to be effective most of the time with children, especially when its important to them (use of the car, attending a concert, etc.). What consequences are there for employees?

The use of Check Back is a fabulous technique that allows your team to accomplish tasks that you assign to them which ultimately strengthens the team and its individual members, both personally and professionally. It has been my experience that when I get out of the way, good things happen!

Six-Step Problem-Solving Method

Whenever our team comes up against a problem or challenge with some aspect of our business, we implement the **Six-Step Problem-Solving Method** that helps us to organize our thoughts, come up with the best solutions, and effectively take action so that we are able to meet our objectives. I am pleased to share it with you.

Step One: Identify the Facts

It is important that everybody on the team understands the facts surrounding the situations that we're about to deal with. Some people call this the **Situation Analysis**. It's also very important that we deal with this on an unemotional basis. Sometimes the passion which people have can get in the way of looking at situations completely on a factual basis. Once we've identified all the facts involved in the problem that we're looking at, we move on to step two.

Step Two: Brainstorm Solutions

Brainstorming is a method of problem-solving and idea-gathering that we use to get information and to get everybody on the team involved. During the brainstorming phase you just want to throw out ideas and see if they stick. Do not judge these ideas as they come out, or make comments in a negative way. This could shut down the flow of information. The time to make decisions will come later. Right now the emphasis should be on **quantity, not quality**.

I was doing a consulting job for McDonnell Douglas in St. Louis, and we were having a brainstorming session with the employees. The company had just come off a ninety-nine-day strike. Some of the union employees weren't feeling very cooperative at the time.

One of the participants became somewhat combative and actually said, "You can't make me talk. I'm not going to participate. You can't make anybody talk." I looked at her, and I said, "Let me ask you a question." I then asked her a question and she gave me an answer. Although she decided that she wasn't going to participate the simple act of me asking her a question triggered a response, and I was able to elicit her position on the issue.

The most important thing to remember when brainstorming is to get everybody involved and the simplest way to do this is by asking open-ended questions. Some examples of open-ended questions are:

- So what's your opinion on this?
- How do you see this playing out in the future?
- If you were in my position, what would you do different?

Each one of these types of questions will elicit a response. Don't get caught asking a question that can only be answered with a yes or a no. You will never understand where the person really stands on a particular issue with such deadend answers.

And remember—in this step, there are no good or bad ideas. There are no dumb questions. Sometimes the most laughable idea when first expressed, ends up as the best idea of all, when more thought has been given to it.

Step Three: Get Consensus

It's important to get a consensus among members of the team in order to get everybody on the same page. It only takes one person to sabotage the team and prevent you from moving forward in a positive way toward accomplishing your goals and objectives.

The method that we use in our organization is called the **Fist-to-Five** consensus decision-making method. When we're trying to get consensus, everybody has got to be in one hundred percent agreement on the direction and solutions that we're going to implement. We won't move forward on our objectives unless everybody is on the same page. Now I know you're probably saying, how are we going to get everybody in one hundred percent agreement on anything. Well, here's how we do it. There is a key phrase that we utilize when we're using consensus decision-making. That key phrase is: **Can You Live with It?**

We know that there are some things in life that people just don't like or want to do. In fact, there are a lot of things in life that I don't like to do. I just know it needs to be done and I make it what I call a non-issue. There is nothing I can do about the situation so I might as well just focus on getting it done. My experience in working with thousands of people over the last twenty years in my professional life, as well as in my personal life, is that most people can live with most things even though they may not like it—as long as it doesn't go against any moral or ethical issues that they have.

When I ask the question, "Can You Live with It?" most people respond in the affirmative. Here's how it works:

Let's say we've been brainstorming on a couple of different issues and everybody in the room has had an opportunity to express their opinion and make their case. The next step is to get consensus. I let everybody know that it's time to get consensus on our plan. It is now up to the members of the team—by a show of hands—to let me know where they stand on the issue. Here are their options:

- **Five fingers** raised means you're in 100% in agreement
- **Four fingers** raised means you're not quite in 100% agreement, but you're not going to prevent the team from moving forward
- **Three fingers** up means you're on the fence
- If you **raise your fist** in the air it means you're 100% against the project

This method will give you an opportunity to get a visual response on where everybody stands on an issue. This will also give you an opportunity to reposition yourself so that you can sell your team on the ideas successfully. By using the fist to five method, each and every person on the team is accepting responsibility by participating and you can now move on to your next step of the problem-solving method.

Step Four: Assign Roles and Responsibilities

During this phase each and every person on the team is assigned a specific role and responsibility. This way, everybody on the team is on the same page and knows where the project stands. This also helps with communication, because when you know who is responsible for a specific task you will have the ability to communicate with them directly. It will help you to streamline information so that you can rapidly respond in a positive way to any challenge that you may face.

Step Five: Explain Expectations

This is the phase where we sit down and explain our expectations to each and every person on the team. Everybody already knows what their roles and responsibilities are and I like to be up front about what I expect from all members of the team. This way, there are no surprises, and it limits the number of issues that employees have with management. By explaining your expectations you will also limit the number of excuses from nonperformance.

Step Six: Check Back

Earlier I discussed the technique that we use for delegation called **Check Back**. In step six the use of Check Back is essential so that we can hold everybody accountable and keep our projects and goals on course. I have used this six-step problem-solving method with small companies and major corporations. It is used by coaches both on the professional and college levels. I know if you implement this six-step problem-solving method, your chances of success will increase and the amount of stress that you're going to go through will substantially decrease.

The Disease Called Constructive Criticism

Growing up I dealt with a lot of so-called "constructive criticism." I know that it was constructive criticism because before anybody ever came up to me, they would always say, "Would you mind if I give you little constructive criticism?" Now I don't know that I'll care or get defensive when people tell me up front that they want to criticize me. I don't think anybody wants to be criticized, and I truly believe that even when we begin to "constructively criticize" people. They close their ears, listen to their own thoughts, and simply don't like you, no matter how well-meaning the criticizer may be!

I prefer to use a different method called "**Like Best, Next Time.**" It's been my experience, through studying success and communication over the years, that when someone makes a mistake, their inner voice starts to speak to them in order to let them know about the mistake. Sometimes people will even beat themselves up for hours over little mistakes. The first thing that the little voice inside them says is, "The next time I'm going to do this differently." They have already figured out what they need to do in order to fix their problem. When this happens, the last thing that they want is someone to come over and beat them over the head with some "constructive criticism."

Generally, when someone figures out their problem for themselves, they don't make the same mistake the second time. So when I'm using the technique Like Best, Next Time, the first thing I do is point out to the individual what I liked best about how they handled the situation. I'm going to find some strength, something that they did well.

Once I focus on my "like best," I then give them my "Next time," otherwise known as the Monday morning quarterback. "What can we learn from this?" "What will we do next time?" I turn the situation around and ask the employee or team member for their Like Best, Next Time.

Again, once they verbalize what they Like Best, they are going to feel better about the situation and it will also help to improve their self-image. When they focus on the Next Time, they end up improving on their future performance and limiting the number of mistakes they make, now and in the future. I have found that when I use the technique of Like Best, Next Time, it keeps me focusing on the positive aspects of the relationship and the solutions needed in order to succeed.

Paraphrasing Your Key to Understanding

In my opinion, there are a number of techniques and skills that you can acquire in order to better communicate with people on a daily basis. However, the number one communication tool that I have seen is called **paraphrasing**. Paraphrasing is simply repeating back to that person in your own words, what you thought you heard them say.

The one individual who is a master at paraphrasing is the interviewer Larry King. Rarely do people turn down a Larry King interview. One of the main reasons is that Larry is a master communicator and the people who go on the Larry King Live television show understand that their message is not going to be twisted or misconstrued. Larry always gets to the bottom of the issue and he does it very simply—by paraphrasing his words.

The way I like to paraphrase is by starting off by making a statement that goes like this: "So what you're saying is..." I then repeat back to the person in my own words what I thought I heard them say. Using this technique accomplishes a couple of things:

(1) The individual I am communicating with will let me know if we are on the same page regarding our communication, and

(2) It gives the individual that I am paraphrasing to, the opportunity to correct me if we are not on the same page.

As I explained earlier, we all hear things differently based on our experiences and our upbringing, otherwise known as our M.F.T.P. The number one reason for disagreements and failure in business and other relationships, is due to a breakdown in communication. Paraphrasing will give you the best opportunity to clarify your communication and convey to the other individual that what they have to say is important, that it means something to you, and that you listened.

That's Not Like You

When my children were growing up I began experimenting with my communication skills and techniques. I had heard that the first word a child learns is the word "no." Some children have been told no so many times that they may even think that their name is "No."

I know I felt like this as a kid growing up. My father would say don't do this and don't do that. No, No, No. It also became apparent to me early on that when people make mistakes they tend to beat themselves up mentally. I have worked in companies and organizations in which people made mistakes, and have been so tough on themselves that they end up crying. I can tell you from experience that when this happens, that person is mentally gone from work for the rest of the day. They might as well just go home because their productivity levels will drop off the face of the earth. Besides that, it's not much fun to have a crying adult in your office or even in your building. It also is disruptive to the entire organization.

In order to avoid some of these mishaps I decided to develop a technique that I could use on my children. My philosophy was, if it worked on them I knew it would work on my employees as well.

When my son Alex, or my daughter Jamie, made a mistake, I could tell that they were taking it very hard and beating themselves up about it. I would say to them, "That's not like you." I then went on to explain to them why it wasn't like them. I didn't want my children to attach the mistake they had made with who they were as individuals. For example, there was a period when my son Alex was younger, that he would forget virtually everything. He would leave his jackets at school or his sneakers at a friend's house. He even forgot whether or not he had homework on a daily basis, if you can believe that.

He was just one of those carefree kids, who didn't seem to have a problem in the world and maybe even lacked a little responsibility. What can you expect, he was only twelve at the time, but I remember the story like it was yesterday. We had just driven back home from the city after staying over at a friend's house for a couple of days. We were getting ready to get in the car because Alex had a basketball game. I asked him where his sneakers were because we needed to get going, or we would be late. He was scurrying around the house looking under his bed, and everywhere imaginable, but he couldn't find them anywhere. Suddenly a light went off in his head and he realized he had left his sneakers at my friend's house, which was over an hour away. He now knew he couldn't go play basketball in a half-hour without the sneakers. He started to say things to himself like, "I'm so dumb, I can't believe I did that, I always forget things." The mind doesn't know the difference between something actually happening and something imagined vividly in great detail.

The last thing that I want my son to start doing is affirming negative ideas and attaching them mentally. This is a surefire way for any individual to lower their self-image. I immediately went into action. I looked at Alex and said, "**That's not like you.**" I then proceeded to tell him why it's not like him, focusing on his strengths. "You're a smart kid, you have a great memory, and I know you didn't do this on purpose." Once I was done building him up and focusing on his strengths, I then implemented the **Next Time technique.** "The next time you have a game, it's important to prepare your equipment the night before, so you can be ready to go." To this day that technique has had a great impact on my son. Today he's a very focused individual with an outstanding memory and a positive mental attitude. Oh yes, he missed that basketball game.

Communication Techniques for Dealing with Difficult People

Have you ever received a telephone call from an irate customer? You know, the person who was just unhappy that day and was going to take everything out on you? I feel it's important to understand that the irate phone caller would've taken out their feelings of anger on anyone. Unfortunately, you just happened to be the one who answered the phone that day. The good news is that there are two techniques I learned a number of years ago that have not only helped me to handle these situations, but have also given me opportunities to turn these situations around in a positive way and create lifelong customers.

I Understand

"**I understand**"—two simple words that can defuse most situations. Most people become upset because they don't think anybody "gets" them. Some of them even believe that they are being picked on, and that these bad things are only happening to them.

In general, I am a pretty controlled individual, and I understand both sides of the customer service coin. I understand what needs to be done as a business owner from a customer service perspective and also as a consumer. An incident happened to me recently, in which the use of "I understand" was used on me by a savvy customer service supervisor at my satellite provider, with great success.

It was Thanksgiving morning and I was really excited because I was having the whole family over for the holiday meal. That morning, my daughter was watching television, when suddenly the day started to look like it could be the best Thanksgiving Day ever. For eighteen years I had one of the original RCA home theater television sets in my home. You know, the ones that weighed about four hundred pounds and had speakers that were five feet tall. Back in 1988 this was the latest technology. It had all the whistles and bells for that day.

Well, for the last three weeks the television set had been on the fritz, and in my world this was a good thing. I had wanted one of those new high definition television sets ever since they came out. The problem was that I couldn't substantiate to my wife our need to buy a new television set since we already had one in every room of the house.

Jamie turned on the television set and all you heard was a popping noise. The television set finally blew up. Boy was I excited! I knew that this was my best opportunity to purchase the television set of my dreams. The next day I proceeded to do something that would lead to hours of frustration and was one of the worst decisions of my life. In fact, maybe you have already experienced this scenario. Have you ever made the decision to go to the shopping malls the day after Thanksgiving? I said I would never become a part of that scene. But that was not until my television set blew up. It was a crazy decision!

For two-and-a-half hours, I drove around the Sawgrass Mills Mall just looking for parking. In the car, my children were asking me every five minutes when was I going to find a parking space. I thought I was going to lose it! Have you ever felt like you could eat your young? I was almost at that point, when suddenly we found a spot.

I was excited and on my way to the store until I saw the line. The store had been closed because of the onslaught of people in the early morning hours. In fact, an elderly lady had been trampled and the videotape was on the news later that night. We left and went home.

The next day I went with my neighbor Barry to Best Buy and I bought one of those Samsung sixty-one inch High Definition television sets, with all the whistles and bells. Mission accomplished. I couldn't wait to get home and plug it in. What I wasn't aware of was the fact that if you did not have a high definition signal the picture on the screen would be worse than on a regular set. I decided at that moment to call my satellite provider and order the high definition satellite dish.

Their customer service representative answered the phone, and I placed my order. She said their technician would be over in two days to install my new satellite dish and TiVo. On the appointed day, I waited around all day for their technician and no one showed up. I went back to my computer to check the order, and it had been canceled.

So I called up the satellite company, explained to them that I had waited around all day and that someone had canceled my order. The customer service representative apologized and reinstituded the order. This happened not once, but four times, and it took me almost sixty phone calls to resolve this issue. Two weeks later, a technician finally came to replace my old satellite dish with a new high definition satellite dish.

That's when I turned into the irate customer. You see, years ago, when I was traveling around the country, staying at exotic resorts in beautiful locations, I had a dream that when I built my new house I was going to build a pool in the backyard that would be a replica of what I had seen many times at those resorts. In fact, this was one of the first things on my goal list when I moved down to Florida years ago. In 2002, when I built my new house I designed my pool and backyard after the ones I had seen years ago.

It's a beautiful pool, shaped like a lagoon with waterfalls and exotic trees of all kinds, including palm trees and coconut trees. It also provides all the privacy you can have in the world. It's my little piece of heaven and I like to keep it that way!

That was until the satellite technician showed up. He walked into the backyard and started to install the new satellite dish, running wires into the house. I suddenly heard a noise. It was the sound of drilling. The technician was drilling a hole from the outside of my house right through my wall to the inside of the house. I was in shock. I yelled out over the sound of the drilling and said, "Stop! What are you doing?" He replied that this was the way that they installed satellite dishes at their company. Impossible, I said. I already have a satellite dish, and they ran the wires through the wall so that they didn't leave any wires exposed.

In addition to that, the technician was also running the big cable directly from the satellite dish around the outside of my gutters onto the roof, which was not only impractical, but it also looked horrible in my beautiful backyard that I had so painstakingly designed.

I immediately ran to the phone to call the satellite provider. I was not interested in speaking to a customer service person this time. I immediately asked for the supervisor and began to explain to them, what had happened since the inception of my order. I wasn't very happy. In fact you could say I was irate. When I finished explaining everything to the supervisor, there was silence. He paused for a second and the first words out of his mouth were, **"I understand how you feel."** I immediately let out a sigh of relief. "Finally, somebody understands how I feel." The supervisor fixed everything. In fact, he gave me a brand-new high definition TiVo player at no charge for all the trouble that I had experienced. The use of the phrase "I understand" is an excellent way to build rapport with people, whether they are customers, friends, family members, or professional athletes. It simply says that you care!

The Three F's

The second technique that I found to be very effective when communicating with someone who is upset is a technique called **The Three F's**. The three F's stand for: **Feel**, **Felt** and **Found**. I learned this technique a number of years ago and have been sharing it with my staff ever since. Let me give you an example: My son was doing great in school. In fact, his best subject is math, and he can basically get A's without really trying. He is very lucky to have this natural ability. He must get it from both of his grandfathers since they both had similar abilities and strengths in that area.

Alex was pretty excited about going on a cruise with the family two days after his final exams. At that time of the year he was doing what most sixteen-year-olds do, and that was focusing on his summer vacation, not focusing on his final exams. As the schedule would have it, his last test of the semester was math. I know he believed that he was going to just slide through the final exam as he had done for most of the year. Well, he was wrong. He wasn't fully prepared, and it was his lowest score of the year. Alex was unaware of his grade on the final exam until he returned from the cruise. I picked him up from the cruise and pulled him aside to show him his report card. He was visibly upset when he got to his math grade and the teacher's comments. The teacher stated that if he had only scored the class average he would have retained his A+ status.

The final exam dropped his grade to a B+. Alex is a highly motivated kid and his top priority was to go to an excellent college. However, his lack of discipline and focus for a very short time diminished the work he had done for an entire year. It was important that I address this issue immediately with him since he had a whole summer in front of him and school was two months away. Anyway, there was nothing he could do about the final exam at this point.

I looked at Alex and said, "I understand how you feel. I have felt that way too." I then related to him an instance from my own life when I experienced the same situation. My lack of focus in a college music course resulted in a failing grade and I had to add additional courses so that I could get my grade point average up again. I then looked at him and said, "I have found that it is much easier to maintain a good grade than it is to make up lost ground." The use of this technique enabled me to accomplish three things.

(1) When I said to Alex, "I understand how you feel," I was building rapport with him on a level that said I care. Remember people want to know that somebody gets them and can relate to their situation.

(2) "I've felt that way too." If misery loves company, this is a surefire way to bond with people. I wanted my son to know that I've been in his position before.

(3) I then related a personal story to use as an example to demonstrate that. The third F is where I gave him the moral of the story. I hoped he would pick up on the lesson. "I found it is much easier to maintain a good grade than to make up for lost ground." This lesson was based on my own real-life experiences.

Every coach who has won the big game, and every manager who has led great teams to victory, have mastered these communication skills. The good news is, because these are skills that can be learned and mastered, all you need to do is to invest some time and **practice**. Soon you'll be a master at communications, and you will have positioned yourself to living a championship life.

LIVING A CHAMPIONSHIP LIFE
ACTION STEP 7:

List Three Instances Where You Could Have Implemented the Lessons That You Have Just Learned in Communication Mastery That Would Have Taken a Negative Situation And Turned It into a Positive Outcome:

1.

2.

3.

CHAPTER 5
PERSISTENCE AND PERSEVERANCE, THE KEYS TO WINNING THE BIG GAME

The best teams in the history of the NFL have won the Super Bowl because they've had two major factors—among others, of course—a **balanced** attack and **persistence**. A balanced attack is common in success stories. The offense supports the defense and vice versa, each having an important role in determining the outcome of the game.

The second factor that has propelled many of these teams to super success is the **persistence and perseverance** of the members of the team, the coaching staffs, and the owners of the organization. If you're a sports fan, you've probably heard a lot about the "drive" that the top athletes in history have had on their way to the top. That "drive" is translated as persistence and perseverance. It separates the winners from losers in, sports and in life.

Recently I read a story in a book called *Successful Achievement*, that was taken from an old newspaper in the early 1950s. It is one of the finest examples of perseverance that I have ever read. Let me share it with you:

"A small boy was learning to skate. His frequent mishaps awaken the pity of a bystander. 'Sonny, you're getting all banged up,' he says. 'Why don't you stop for a while and just watch the others?' With tears still rolling down his cheeks from his last fall, the boy looked from his advisor to the shining steel on his feet and said: 'Mister, I didn't get these skates to give up with; I got them to learn how with!'"

In order for a strong desire to be transformed into reality it must be backed with persistency until it is taken over by your subconscious mind. It is not enough to just feel deeply about your desire for achievement of your goal for only a few hours or a few days, and then forget all about that desire. Your desires must be placed in your mind and held there with persistence that knows no defeat, until your subconscious mind takes it over.

The 1999 Super Bowl champion St. Louis Rams had just that mindset. The Rams reshaped their team in the off-season through trades and the free agency signing of Marshall Faulk and Trent Green. In the third preseason game of the season, Green, who showed promise in the first two games as the starting quarterback, suffered a season-ending knee injury, forcing the Rams to change direction once again.

To replace Green, the Rams called on backup quarterback Kurt Warner, who had never started an NFL game in a career that featured tours in NFL Europe and Arena Football. Going into the season with an unknown quarterback, many experts thought the Rams were in for their tenth straight losing season. They also believed that Dick Vermeil was a lame-duck coach, whose time had passed him by. With their high-powered offense and stellar defense, the Rams got off to a fast start. Led by Kurt Warner, the Rams won their first three games while scoring one hundred points. The perennial losers started to believe in themselves, and it showed. This football team was ready to make their season exciting. They were dubbed the Greatest Show on Turf, and they were going to prove it to everybody.

After four losing seasons, they began to believe in themselves and what they were capable of accomplishing. Still, many of the experts didn't believe that the Rams were for real. They were set to play the San Francisco 49ers, a team that exposed them as phonies in the past and a team they had not beaten regularly over nine years. The Rams not only won the game, it was not even close. The Rams ran over the aging 49ers 42-20, forcing people to take notice of the Rams and their unknown quarterback.

Having an opportunity to be around the players and treating them exposed me to many insights and allowed me to have the opportunity to watch them grow personally and professionally. There was one player however that I had the opportunity to get to know closely, who is an outstanding example of persistence and perseverance—number 52, Michael Jones.

I got to know Mike intimately as a board member on his foundation that conducted free football camps around the country for inner-city kids. If you don't know who Michael Jones is, let me explain. Michael is the player known for one of the greatest plays in Super Bowl history. The play is simply known as "The Tackle." With 2:15 remaining in the game, the Tennessee Titans scored to tie the game. The game appeared to be heading into overtime, when suddenly the Rams struck back with a seventy-three-yard pass from Kurt Warner to Isaac Bruce, to give the Rams a 23-16 lead with 1:54 remaining. However, the game was far from over as the Titans drove down the field with time winding down. The Titans would have one last chance to tie the game. They set up on the Rams seven-yard line with seven seconds left.

The Titans quarterback stepped back into the pocket, and found Kevin Dyson on the three with a perfect pass. He appeared to be waltzing in for a game-tying touchdown, when Mike pulled him down inches from the goal line as time ran out. The St. Louis Rams were Super Bowl champions. Kurt Warner completed his journey from unknown to Super Bowl MVP, and Dick Vermeil retired with his elusive Super Bowl trophy in his hand.

Mike also had a superb performance during the regular season that year, recording one sack and four interceptions which he returned for ninety-six yards and two touchdowns. He also recovered two fumbles, returning them for fifty-one yards and a touchdown.

Mike is a very modest and soft-spoken man. Even after making the great tackle, he exclaimed, "It was a total team effort." A native of Kansas City, Missouri, Mike was not considered one of the top high school players in the nation when he played for Southwest High School. Jones attended college at the University of Missouri where he played running back.

National Football League teams passed over Jones in the 1991 draft, an embarrassment that bothered him for years. He was eventually signed as a free agent by the Los Angeles Raiders who sent him to the Sacramento Surge of the World League in 1992, to gain experience. But over the next four years Jones earned a reputation as a hustler known for making big plays on the Raiders special teams. Eventually Mike made his way to the starting line-up as a linebacker. When his contract with the Raiders expired, he signed with St. Louis, the hometown of his wife Leslie, whom he met in college.

Mike grew up in a tough neighborhood on East 76th Street in Kansas City. He was the fifth of nine children and his parents were married for fifty-five years. His father, Leroy, who recently passed away, was a mail clerk at the U. S. Post Office for forty years. His mother worked as a clerk for the Internal Revenue Service. They were not poor, but his parents could never afford to send Jones to football camps run by professional players.

His neighborhood was the type of place where some young men did not make it to adulthood. Mike succeeded in football and one of his closest friends became a lawyer. But he had other friends who ended up in jail. His closest friend, Kenny White, served time in prison and then was shot and killed in a gun battle on Valentine's Day, 1993. This tragedy prompted Mike to start a foundation that gives scholarships each year to underprivileged students in Kansas City and St. Louis.

He also conducts free football camps for impoverished teenage athletes in Missouri and Illinois, and has an annual golf tournament in order to raise funds to put on more camps and charitable events in the future. Mike says he owes his dogged determination and persistence and perseverance that sustained him in the NFL, to his grandfather, William Baker. Baker never went beyond fourth grade in school, but taught himself advanced mathematics and engineering. He also taught himself and his nine grandchildren how to play the piano. Mike once said that, "his grandfather tried to instill greatness in his kids, and that his mother tried to instill it in him." His example of persistence and perseverance should be a guide to all of us if we want to Live a Championship Life.

Persistence and perseverance are important if we want to win the big game. However, winning the big game is not as enjoyable as you might think, unless you have people to share it with. When you share your life with others, you add balance to your life and the number of victories that you can achieve is infinite.

CHAPTER 6
FAITH, FORGIVENESS, AND GRATITUDE—THE BUILDING BLOCKS TO SUCCESS

I t is my belief that there are three essential building blocks that one must possess in order to build a foundation for success and balance in their life. Those building blocks are **Faith, Forgiveness, and Gratitude.** Napoleon Hill, the famous author of *Think and Grow Rich*, said, "Faith involves a principle that is so far reaching into fact that no man can say what its limitations are or if it has any limitations."

Faith

All human beings are born with an internal mechanism that provides them with inherent faith as a natural universal principle. It is only outside forces that cause people to discount faith. We need faith every day just to get out of bed in the morning, to walk across the street, and to lie down at night, knowing that we will rise the next day.

Faith is the foundation of all success in life. Without faith there is no life and no reason to live. We must have faith that we were born on this earth for a purpose and that our life's quest is to discover that purpose and embrace it to serve our fellow man. Our faith grows in direct proportion to the amount we are tested in life. We must be willing to have faith that our failures in life will eventually lead us to an even greater success.

In writing this book, I am currently witnessing within myself and others around me how our faith is tested. The universe will always throw a roadblock in your way in order to stretch your boundaries of faith and to let it grow even stronger. Faith is built stronger by prayer and the knowledge that there is a higher power in the universe that works through each one of us in harmony with nature.

Faith is with us for the long haul. It's not to be used for instant gratification.

The person who says to the universe, if you just let me have this I promise to be good, shows little knowledge of true faith. But the person who works towards a definite chief aim with the knowledge that he or she will eventually achieve his or her goals without a time limit placed on such goals, shows the true, endless limits of faith, and they will always achieve their results even if it takes many years.

Faith knows no religion or bounds, and is in each and every one of us. It only needs to be exercised. There are many instances throughout history, where mankind has shown considerable reserves of faith in the struggle for success.

One instance that comes to my mind is the story of Scott O'Grady. Scott was a pilot who was flying a reconnaissance mission over Bosnia, when his plane was shot down. He was alone on the ground in Bosnia for several days and was constantly hiding in fear for his life. If he was found, he would surely have been killed. Scott, however, used all his abilities and training and directed them with faith—faith so strong in himself and God that he even said he had visions of the Virgin Mary. It was with all those powerful reserves of faith and belief that he was able to survive. He was finally rescued by U.S. Marines in the Bosnian forest. Scott used his faith to give him inner strength and to survive the crisis.

Another story that comes to mind from the military is the one of Captain Gerald Coffee who was shot down while flying a combat mission over North Vietnam. Much of his seven years and nine days as a Prisoner of War was spent in solitary confinement. The only thing that helped him to survive, he said, was his faith and belief that one day he would be released and see his family again. These are but two examples of men who have used their faith to accomplish their goals.

My life has been an exercise of faith in progress. I started to write this book in 1995 when the Los Angeles Rams moved to St. Louis. At the time I was going through a divorce and I felt like my world was crashing down around me. However, the one thing that I knew was that I had to cling onto some seed of faith, no matter how big or how small. I knew there was a lesson to be learned out of this unfortunate situation.

Maybe the loss of so many things that I cherished, was actually a gift in disguise. At the time I was certain of one thing, that faith without a definite chief aim or goal would not end in positive results and would not improve my situation.

For example: a car that leaves New York with a destination of Los Angeles likely will not get to its destination, if there is no map. You will not end up at your destination either if you don't have a definite chief aim or goal, and a roadmap to get there. Because of that, I decided to place my faith in the internal knowledge that my life had a purpose and a reason. This reason and purpose I believed was to help others. I wasn't quite sure at the time about how I was going to do it or how it would unfold.

On June 13, 1996 I received a call from my good friends, Kathy and Tony, informing me that there was a window of opportunity to work with a company and their team of individuals in this corporation that was interviewing the following week. The company was called AT&T and the product was the 1-800 Imagine Line. On Friday, June 21, 1996 I was informed that I was a leading candidate for the opportunity, and later that night I received a telephone call and was told I had been selected.

This was my stepping stone into the world of large corporations. I believed there was no coincidence in this opportunity presenting itself at the time it did. For nearly three months I had constant faith and determination that an opportunity would present itself and now I could see some light at the end of the tunnel.

Although faith is important it is only one of the components that make up the success triad.

In order for you to achieve your goals and be successful, another step needs to be taken. I'm talking about **forgiveness**.

Forgiveness

It was once said that, "Those who can't forgive others break the bridge over which they must pass themselves in order to have their lives work." Faith is not enough, it is only one step. Forgiveness was a big step for me, as I'm sure it will be for you or anyone you know who's been hurt. I grew up in a very strict household, where sometimes physical and mental abuse was the norm. Because of this I harbored a lot of resentment against my parents and, in turn, linked that to the predicament I was presently facing.

Then one day I heard a speaker named Mike Wickett say, "A person can only act in accordance with the way they learned as a child." What he was saying was that our parents did the best job they knew how to do. I am not stating this to make anyone feel bad that is not in a good marriage or who has a poor relationship with their family or friends. All I'm saying is they probably did the best job they could with the skills they had at the time. If we can understand this concept, and "forgive them for they know not what they do," then we will be able to lift a great burden from ourselves and be able to move on with our lives in a positive direction.

Resentment and the inability to forgive others is a cancer that will affect the mind and body in various ways, slowly killing each and every one of us. I'm not saying that this is easy to do. For me one of the toughest things I've ever had to do was to forgive certain family members for things they'd done to me. That's before I was introduced to a theory called **Blocked Energy**.

Blocked Energy

The theory of Blocked Energy states that when you resent or dislike others, the natural energy that exists in the universe is unable to flow through you, thus impeding your life. Until we forgive people we will not be able to carry on and accomplish our mission in life. However, once we forgive others that have hurt us, we will be open to the universal laws of nature that would not only give us great reserves of energy, but will also enable us to unblock and be open to the state of grace that surrounds us daily.

Just the other day I was in a bookstore, and I noticed a bookmark that said, "**Those that we resent live rent free in our heads**." Wow! Another way to look at that is: if we resent and dislike other people, they own us. If you're like me, this has probably happened to you. You're driving down the highway and someone cuts your car off, and your blood starts to boil. Maybe this is something that upsets you for hours. In the past I would have felt the same way. But this might have been an innocent incident. The driver of the other car might not even have been aware that this happened. They might have had some serious problems or some bad news they were wrestling with, or even were on their way to the emergency room.

But right now the other person probably is sitting on the beach getting a good tan or getting on with his or her life, and we are still upset and still thinking about what happened. In that instance they own us mentally and are living rent free in our head. It's important to get past this mode of thinking. How about this possibility—maybe you were just being tested to see if you could handle the situation.

Each and every event in our lives happens for a reason and a purpose. If we can make it our life's quest to find out why, we will get closer to being healthier and happier every day.

The essence here is to forgive others and allow a major burden to be lifted from our lives. But this is only half of the equation. The other half is that we must forgive ourselves, too, because this is the healthiest thing that we can do in order to balance our lives.

If you tend to beat yourself up, stop it! When the outside world is trying to beat you up and put you down, you do not need to add to the battle. We're not perfect; no one is. The only way that we can strive for some semblance of perfection is from making mistakes. Yes, that's right, failure is the key. No man or woman has ever been successful without first failing in some aspect of their lives.

Time and time again, I've seen people who have had a failed marriage, make their next one a success. I know people who have gone bankrupt, then turn around and make a fortune. Maybe this is just part of the learning process that we humans must go through in order to be successful. The saying that in every failure there is a seed or embryo of success has never been truer.

It was once said that "Failure teaches men lessons which they would never learn without it. Among the great lessons taught by failure is that of humility."

So stop beating yourself up. Give yourself a break. You're not always going to be right. However, if you can recognize this and make some corrections, you will be on the road to living a championship life

If you're still not sure about the best way to forgive yourself and forgive others, let me share with you a technique that I think you will find very helpful.

The Forgiveness Letter

The **Forgiveness Letter** is an excellent technique to use when forgiving yourself or others. The first step is to write a letter to all the people that you need to forgive. These letters should leave no stone unturned—forgive others completely for everything, no matter what. There is a catch to this that you should know about, which might alleviate some of the stress in following through on this technique. Step two—you don't necessarily have to mail these letters to those people. The process of just writing them alone will remove a great burden from you, and it will help you move on with the healing process.

Gratitude

The last leg of our triad that will put you on the road to living a championship life is **Gratitude**. When you are grateful for the things that you have in your life you will have less fear and stress. Each and every day I wake up and go for a walk so that I can spend at least five minutes, visualizing and focusing on everything and everyone in my life that I appreciate.

As I'm walking I sometimes close my eyes, if I'm on the beach or somewhere where it's okay to do so. I'll just imagine the specific people that I love in my life and that I'm really grateful for. I start with a spiral outside of myself and list all the things I'm grateful for.

For instance I start by saying to myself how, "I'm grateful for my own life and I'm grateful for my health and the choices that I have and the knowledge that I can use." Then I start thinking about my children, and next I start thinking about my wife and my family members. I then move on to my friends and business associates.

The more you can think about, and visualize the specific people and situations that you are grateful for, the better you're going to feel. If you want to strengthen these feelings of gratitude when you're doing this exercise, try walking and visualizing the looks on the faces of those for whom you are grateful. Also, if you say these thoughts out loud, and repeat them over and over, it will strengthen your belief system.

I am so grateful for my health!
I am so grateful for my health!
I am so grateful for my health!

At the minimum say it in your mind over and over.
I'm so grateful for my wife and I love her so much!
I'm so grateful for Alex. He is such a great son, I love him so much!
I am so grateful for my daughter, Jamie. I love her so much. She's such a sweet and kind person!

When I practice this exercise I think about each and every one of these people and instances specifically about them and what

I'm grateful for. If you're in a place right now, you might be saying to yourself, "But I'm not grateful." If that's the case, then turn around and ask yourself these questions:

- If I could be grateful, what would I be grateful for?
- What are the things in my life that I could be grateful for?
- What are the opportunities in my life that I could be grateful for?
- Who are the people in my life that I could be grateful for? For what situations?
- Simply—What are you most grateful for?

By doing this you will be able to diminish your fears, get rid of stress, and become much happier. I've met many people who seem to have everything! Unfortunately they are unfulfilled—they're fearful and stressed out because they're not grateful. On the other hand, I've met so many people that seem to have little or nothing, and yet they're happy and grateful. When you are grateful you are rich. When you are ungrateful, and you're not appreciative, you're stressed, you're poor, and you're frustrated. Which would you rather be?

When we are grateful we tend to focus on what's right about our lives and our relationships with others. Practicing gratitude on a daily basis has helped me to mend fences and raise happy and healthy children with my ex-wife, Laurie. So many children who come from divorced families end up having extra challenges in life. But because of the gratitude and appreciation I have for the mother of my children, we've been able to overcome many of the obstacles that divorced families face. The triad of **Faith**, **Forgiveness**, and **Gratitude**—when implemented—can be one of your most powerful tools in attaining your goals and dreams, and living a championship life.

CHAPTER 7
LIFE BALANCE

LIFE BALANCE

Life Balance is critical to your emotional balance. If you're going to have a Championship Life, you must have balance in your personal, as well as your professional lives. All the goals and all the success in the world won't make up for the hopes and dreams that many people miss out on by not having balance in their lives.

Creating magic moments

It's important to take time out for yourself and to plan time to spend with your family members and friends. My goal with my children for the last seventeen years has been to create moments that they will remember forever. Recently I was in Costa Rica with my family, and for many weeks I had been planning on how to create a moment with my daughter, Jamie, since we don't spend as much time together as I do with her brother, Alex.

My friend Bob Pollack has a condominium overlooking a beach called Playa Blanca, which is one of the most beautiful beaches in all of Costa Rica. He lets us stay at his place a lot, which my family and I are grateful for. (And I tell him so, too.) The beach is absolutely magnificent, with tall mountains in the background, Scarlet Macaws flying overhead, and hundreds of different types of fish swimming around the reefs. Knowing that Jamie is the first to arise every morning I decided that I just wanted to take a walk along the beach with her and spend some private time.

As you might imagine, being twelve at the time she was more interested in watching the Disney Channel than taking a walk on the beach at 7:30 in the morning. Finally, after much convincing, she agreed to go with me on a walk down the beach. It was a magnificent day and a magnificent sight. We saw exotic birds, monkeys swinging from the trees, crabs running up on the beach, and turtles laying eggs. We walked out on the rocks where the ocean met the sand and watched the ocean crash along the rocks.

My goal and objective to create a magic moment for that trip was now complete. I created a moment that my daughter—and I—will remember for a lifetime. Many things will happen to you on your journey throughout this lifetime. However, when it's all said and done, the moments—especially special moments—of our lives are the ones that we will hold most precious.

Two of my closest mentors have been my grandparents. We call them Mimi and Pop. They both have been a shining example in my life and a testament to the importance of creating moments. I remember fondly to this day the times that they would take me fishing, or the times I was playing drums on the top of their folding tables, and especially the time my grandmother took me to Friendly's for a cheeseburger. I also remember the lessons that they taught me, especially the life lessons that I now share with my children. The greatest gift that you can give another person is when you share a piece of yourself.

Health and its importance in becoming a champion

It almost goes without saying that all the factors that contribute to living a Championship Life are almost worthless if you do not have good mental and physical health. Our bodies and minds are our vehicles for success and we need to take exceptional care not to waste our two prime assets. It has been my experience in almost twenty years of practice that most people take better care of their cars than they do of their own bodies. The good news is that there are a number of relatively easy steps that we can take in order to put ourselves in the optimum physical and mental condition so that we can achieve all of our goals. As a chiropractor I believe in the total body approach to health. Every day we are faced with outside stresses from the environment on our body and the stress that we impose on ourselves through poor diet and exercise. These are generally correctable factors if we follow some simple guidelines.

Rethink what you eat. There is a myth that has been going around that I would like to dispel. The myth is: if you exercise, it doesn't matter what you eat. The fact is, if you exercise it matters even more what you eat. Americans are exercising more now than ever before. However we still see a rapid rise in the number of Americans who are obese and who are suffering from health problems caused by being unfit. The fact of the matter is that physically active individuals need more nutrients than their sedentary counterparts. So it's important that you eat a healthy diet.

One of the rules that we have for our patients is: Avoid the Three Whites; flour, sugar, and salt. They have little nutritional value, and their regular intake will eventually break down your body. It's also important to understand that mom was right! Breakfast is the most important meal of the day. It's the gasoline for our car and the energy for our body. When we miss breakfast we are forcing our body to go into starvation mode, which will diminish our energy throughout the day.

The second most important meal of the day is lunch, which should also be the largest meal of the day. Finally, there is dinner, which should be the smallest meal of the day, because whatever is not digested by the time we go to bed generally will turn into fat. If you're really interested in eating right, I suggest that you eat five mini meals a day. If you've ever been on a Weight Watchers diet plan or Jenny Craig or any of the other diet plans out there. you'll notice that they are always set up with three meals and two snacks, which would equal your five small meals a day.

Exercise daily and in moderation. Let's take a look at another myth: the longer you exercise the better. The fact is, too much exercise prevents results. I learned from countless hours of research—personal experience in working with professional athletes—that working out too much actually will take you further away from your goals. Not only is it hard on the body but is also very draining on your mind. By doing brief intense and highly effective workouts that stimulate the muscles and burn fat, you can accomplish your goals and stay in shape in less than four hours a week.

There is one more myth that needs to be addressed in order for us to understand exercise and weight loss better. The myth is that aerobics is better for shaping up than weight training. The fact is, in order to transform your body you must train with weights. Yes, walking around the block or simply climbing a flight of stairs is better than just sitting there doing nothing. But the best form of exercise for reshaping your body is weight training through resistance training. It can significantly increase your metabolic rate, which is the rate at which your body burns fat. As you may already know, when you gain muscle your body requires more energy to maintain that new muscle. Fat weight doesn't require any energy at all to maintain—it just sits there. That's why weight training is even superior to aerobic exercise for people who want to lose fat. It addresses the core of the problem—the rate at which your body uses energy. Having a regular exercise program will put you in a position that will enable you to accomplish all your goals and objectives for years to come.

Minimize pressure and handle stress with relaxation techniques

Whether you are a student or an athlete or a leader in business or just maybe a mom or a dad, you must have techniques that are going to help you to minimize pressure and handle stress.

Breathe right. Don't forget to breathe! When we are under stress our breathing pattern tends to change, becoming shallow, and you feel more pressured. Just practice! That is all you have to do. Here is an exercise that you can try: close your eyes a second and take a big breath inside your nose and blow it out through your mouth. Keep blowing until all of the air is out, and take another big breath in through your nose and let it all the way out, through your mouth. When you do this you'll start to notice that you feel a little more relaxed, your shoulders and deep breathing slows down, and relaxes you.

There is another technique you can do called a One Minute Countdown, which will also help you relax. Simply take a moment and start to count, saying: one thousand ninety-nine, one thousand ninety-eight, etc. Continue this for at least one minute. As you're doing this, you relax different parts of your body from your head down to your toes. It takes a bit of practice but it is worth the effort. It's just a simple form of meditation. Experts say fifteen minutes of meditation is equivalent to almost eight hours of sleep.

Guided imagery. Guided Imagery is another relaxation technique. It involves thinking back to a time when you were totally relaxed—when there was no stress in your body whatsoever. When you take yourself back to that point in time, you can relive that experience. It will energize you every time. Guided Imagery works best with tapes or CDs. You can find Guided Imagery tapes online or at your local discount stores. There are CDs with sounds of nature, or which talk you through relaxation experiences. Both work well.

Reading to reduce stress, and inspire. Reading not only gives you knowledge, it also is a fantastic stress reliever—that is as long is you're not reading something like Stephen King novels. Develop the practice of reading early in the morning—especially inspirational subjects—and before you go to sleep. It will not only relax you, but it will also give you ideas that will stick with you for much longer periods of time. When you regularly feed your mind with inspirational and motivational information, you will be inspired and motivated in everything you do.

Create a schedule for daily stress reduction. Make sure that you schedule leisure time. Committing to leisure time is just as important as committing to work time. We are only on this planet for a short period of time. And I never met anyone who was in a hospital bed, who thought they should spend more time at the office. So go out and play, have fun, and enjoy yourself. After all, don't you deserve it?

And on that same note, schedule family and spouse or significant other time. Make a date with your wife or husband at least once a week. Yes, hire a baby-sitter if you need to, but get away for some one-on-one sharing and intimacy in order to keep a spark in your relationship. In like manner, take time to make memories with your children (remember my walk on the beach with my daughter?). These should include not only their scheduled sporting events, concerts, recitals, etc., but also for unscheduled kite-flying and frisbee-throwing jaunts in the park.

Get regular chiropractic adjustments. Your spine and your nervous system are the Mission Control Center for your body. In order to live a Championship Life, it helps that your spine and nervous system are fine-tuned for success. Regular chiropractic adjustments will help to alleviate the stress that we put on our spine every day as we reach for our goals and objectives.

In addition to a maintenance regimen of chiropractic care, the use of Massage Therapy will also aid in restoring your spine to optimal health. Today, most chiropractic offices are multidisciplinary practices, where you can receive all the care you need in just one easy visit.

Learn to laugh

If you work as hard as I do—and I'm sure you do or you wouldn't be reading this book—you need to go out and have fun and learn how to laugh. You know, one of those big old belly laughs, where the tears are flowing down your cheeks and your stomach hurts. This kind of laughing is therapeutic. In fact, Dr. Norman Cousins who wrote several books about laughter and healing, including Anatomy of an Illness As Perceived by the Patient, developed a technique called Laugh Therapy. He became very sick, was told that he had cancer, and that he should just go home and spend his last days with his family. They told Norman he only had three months to live when he left the hospital. So Norman did something quite unusual. He checked himself into a hotel and rented comedy movies like the Keystone Kops, the Three Stooges, the Marx Brothers, and Laurel and Hardy. He watched all the comedians that were big in his day. To cut to the bottom line, Norman lived for almost another three decades, sharing his Laugh Therapy with cancer patients around the world. Cousins said: "Laughter is inner jogging." What a great way to describe it!

So the next time you feel a little stressed, remember back to a time when you were laughing so hard that you couldn't stand it. Right after that moment you will feel totally relaxed and at peace. There is no better stress reliever than laughing. So take the opportunity to go to a comedy club or rent a funny movie and laugh legal. This is a pretty funny world when you think about it. And when you learn to laugh, you will notice the positive effects it will have on you immediately.

By following some of these simple tips, techniques, and lessons you'll start to notice that you are less stressed and your life is more and more balanced. You'll be poised to begin to "Live a Championship Life."

By writing this book, my hope and dreams are for you to attain everything you ever hope for and wish for in life. It's also important that you enjoy your journey on the road to success because it will pass before you know it. I only hope and pray that the lessons that I've shared with you will contribute in some small way, so that you can be happier and healthier, and that you will be living—and winning in—a Championship Life

INDEX

Dr. Rick Goodman Gets Great Results

Dr. Rick Goodman speaks from real-life experiences and achieves great results! Rick has worked with companies of all sizes, from small businesses and entrepreneurial startups to Fortune 500 companies. His high-energy content, rich keynotes, seminars, and workshops are designed for associations and firms of all sizes that want to maximize their potential.

After developing one of the largest healthcare practices in St. Louis, Missouri, Dr. Rick formed Goodman Presentations, a consulting company designed to provide physicians with specific tools and systems, enabling them to grow their practices and rapidly achieve financial independence.

In 1995, Dr. Rick became a medical staff member for two professional sports teams, the St. Louis Rams and the St. Louis Ambush. Soon after, Dr. Rick sold his medical practice and founded a new company called S.T.A. Consulting, Inc., whose primary mission was to introduce his team-building concepts and systems into the corporate sector.

Dr. Rick was then hired by two of the largest corporations in America, McDonnell Douglas and Boeing Corporation. He implemented his proprietary strategies on forming and executing self-directed work teams in all of their production facilities.

Throughout this project, Dr. Rick had the opportunity to work directly with leaders from all branches of the armed services. Their goal was to increase the productivity of their employees, maximize efficiency, and cut costs. In the first two years the program saved each of the companies several million dollars and prevented layoffs at all of their facilities.

In March of 2000, Dr. Rick became vice-president of operations for Neurology Associates Group, Inc., where he helped the company grow from two multi-disciplinary medical facilities to eleven facilities in just three years. His success made Neurology Associates Group one of the largest medical practices in south Florida with more than one hundred employees and revenues in excess several million dollars per year.

Dr. Rick's latest startup is Advantage Legal Seminars. The company was formed in 2005 and is now one of the fastest growing continuing education companies in its field. Advantage offers a full lineup of business and legal themed seminars and products and is currently approved for Continuing Legal Education (CLE) credits in more than twenty-two states. Dr. Rick is a member of the National Speakers Association (NSA), the International Federation for Professional Speakers (IFPS), and is a board member of the Florida Speakers Association (FSA).

Whether delivering a keynote address or a full-day program, Dr. Rick gives your audiences specific tools and systems that enable them to achieve great results. For more about Dr. Rick or to retain his services to speak to your company, visit www.drrickgoodman.com.

Other Products by Rick Goodman

Audio Programs:
Striving for Excellence "What We Do and the People We Touch." CD/DVD
Living a Championship Life "A Game Plan for Success" Audio Book
Winning Strategies for Dealing with Difficult People CD /MP3
How to Run a More Productive Legal Practice CD/MP3
Professionalism and Ethics for Today's Legal Practice CD/MP3

Self-Study Programs
Living a Championship Life 27 Day E-Mail Mini-Course

Training Programs
Success Strategies Determining Your Primary Goals
The Telephone: Your First Impression for Success.
Negotiate to Win "The Art of Successful Negotiations"
Developing Great Leaders That Get Great Results
Winning Strategies for Dealing with Difficult People
It's All about the Customer "How to Grow and Retain Your Customer Base."
Manage your Time and Maximize Your Life
Change Management
Conflict Management

Keynote Speeches
Striving for Excellence "What We Do and the People We Touch"
Living a Championship Life "a game plan for success"
Developing Great Leaders That Get Great Results
Leadership in Action
You! The Real Prescription for Health!

For More Information:

Dr. Rick Goodman
S.T.A. Consulting Inc.
7247 Northwest 22nd Drive
Pembroke Pines, FL 33024

Ph: (888) 267-6098
Fax: (954) 983-2339

E-Mail: Rick@DrRickGoodman.com
www.DrRickGoodman.com

Made in the USA
Middletown, DE
10 June 2015